The Spirit Moves

A Handbook of Dance and Prayer

by Carla De Sola

The Liturgical Conference

The Spirit Moves
A Handbook of Dance and Prayer

by Carla De Sola

 The Liturgical Conference · 1221 Massachusetts Avenue, N.W. · Washington, D.C. 20005

The Spirit Moves—A Handbook of Dance and Prayer is the sixth manual in The Liturgical Conference's ministries series: guidebooks designed for the training, formation and direction of persons entrusted by ecclesial communities with specific liturgical ministries. The ministries series is recommended particularly to clergy, theological and seminary students, pastoral teams, parish liturgy committees, persons involved in liturgical ministries and persons responsible for training for those ministries. This particular volume is offered in a special way to religious educators, for use in their classes and other faith-sharing groups, and to students and teachers of dance, in the hope that it will serve as an invitation to them to bring their gifts to the prayer-life of the churches.

Previous volumes in this series are:

Strong, Loving and Wise—Presiding in Liturgy, by Robert W. Hovda

Liturgy Committee Handbook—A Nine Week Study Guide, edited by Virginia Sloyan

The Lector's Guide—A Four Week Training Program, edited by Gabe Huck and Virginia Sloyan

There Are Different Ministries—Guide for Acolytes, Ministers of Communion, Ushers and Occasional Ministers, by Robert W. Hovda

The Ministry of Music—A Guide for the Practicing Church Musician, by William A. Bauman.

ISBN 0-918208-04-1
Library of Congress Catalog Card Number 77-89743

Cover design by Frank Kacmarcik.
Cover photograph and photographs of Carla De Sola on pages viii, 8, 34, 124, and 146 by Beverly Hall.
Photographs, taken at Georgetown University, on pages 20 and 94 by William Auth.
Photograph, taken at Princeton Liturgical Week (1975), on page 112 by *The Philadelphia Inquirer*.

Table of Contents

ACKNOWLEDGEMENTS

Many resources have been drawn upon in the preparation of this book. The author and publisher wish to express their deep thanks to the publishers, composers and writers of these resources, and to acknowledge the following copyrights:

"The Canticle of Brother Sun" from the album *Sons of the Morning* by Leo Nestor, © 1970, World Library Publications, Inc. Reprinted with permission.

"We See the Lord" by James E. Byrne, © 1971, James E. Byrne.

From "Spirit of the Living God" by Daniel Iverson, copyright 1935, 1963. Moody Press, Moody Bible Institute of Chicago. Used by permission.

The songs "Are Not Our Hearts" and "Hymn of Praise" by Rev. Carey Landry are reprinted by permission of North American Liturgy Resources. All Rights Reserved. Printed sheet music, stereo albums and tapes of this music may be obtained at better religious bookstores or directly from North American Liturgy Resources, 2110 West Peoria Avenue, Phoenix, Arizona 85029. Catalog upon request.

Psalm 115 from *The Psalms: A New Translation* published by William Collins Sons & Co. Ltd. and Collins + World is used by permission of the Grail, England.

Poem by Thomas Merton. All Rights Reserved. Reprinted by permission of New Directions Publishing Corporation.

"All Along The Way" from the Album *Listen,* copyright 1973, The Benedictine Foundation of the State of Vermont, Weston, VT.

English translation of excerpts from the *Roman Missal.* Copyright © 1973, International Committee on English in the Liturgy, Inc. All rights reserved.

Scriptural quotations in this book, unless otherwise noted, are from the Revised Standard Version of the Bible, copyrighted 1946, 1952 © 1971, 1973, by the Division of Education and Ministry, National Council of the Churches of Christ in the U.S.A.

Introduction

The dance-prayers included here are structured and nonstructured. They are for nondancers seeking to take their first steps in movement meditation, and for those with training who need help in applying their technical background to prayer. They are for those needing guidance in leading a congregation into movement, and for those wanting only to pray more freely in their own living-rooms. The dance-prayers ebb and flow, rise and fall, circle and process, moving out of stillness into all life. They can be added upon and they can be subtracted from—they are adaptable to your own experience.

The Spirit Moves—A Handbook of Dance and Prayer is a collection of the articles I have written from 1972-1976 for The Liturgical Conference's periodicals, *Liturgy* and *Major Feasts and Seasons*. They were written to fulfill a need of the church for dance material for both individual and communal prayer.

You have a desire to pray, yet there are no words. Perhaps the Holy Spirit, groaning within his temple, your body (1 Corinthians 6), is teaching you a new language. We read in Isaiah that the word of the Lord does not return empty. It runs through the earth and heavens, changing, moving, taking flesh. Sacred dance is an enfleshment of the spirit in movement to God. The dance begins in the heart. The Holy Spirit is the dancer and Christ is the partner. The dimensions of the dance are endless.

> I was glad when they said to me,
> "Let us go to the house of the Lord!" —Psalm 122

Sometimes I close my eyes and see the reverberations of waves of arms rising, and torsos bending. They are the movements of the church in prayer.

Reflections on Dance and Prayer

Let me begin with a prayer:

I pray that everyone, sitting cramped inside a pew, body lifeless, spine sagging and suffering, weary with weight and deadness, will be given space in which to breathe and move, will be wooed to worship with beauty and stillness, song and dance—dance charged with life, dance that lifts up both body and spirit, and we will be a holy, dancing, loving, praying and praising people.

How can this be done? Does dance really play such a part in worship—such a fragile yet earthy, ephemeral but enduring, peripheral and seemingly useless form of energy in this age of efficient activity?

What is dance? What is its source of strength? Why is it feared and loved? And when did it begin?

The source

All of life involves movement, and movement becomes dance when there is an inner life, a living spirit directing it. A tree gets its energy from the earth and sunlight all around it; the energy isn't just in the sap flowing up and down inside it. In the same way, dance isn't just mechanized intellectuality or rootless flutterings. True dance draws its strength from the living flow of the universe. (Either the universe doesn't hold together and we're simply mad, or we really are connected in some way!) With this power, dance can lead us to the heart of reality; it can turn energy loose within us, and this could be a fearsome thing if one were not rooted in good. The dance began in the beginning, in silence and stillness, as the world lay worshiping under the hand of God, for "the Spirit of God was moving over the face of the waters." The dance began with God!

Movement abounded, for life was bursting forth everywhere. There were the rotation of the planets around the sun, the changing

1

of seasons and of day to night, the creepings of cells and plants and animals; but as yet the dance was incomplete, for it required the human soul—the soul of persons moving in relationship to God—to give this dance its deepest purpose, that of praise and gratitude.

" . . . Then [he] breathed into his nostrils the breath of life; and man became a living being." Made in the image of God—body and spirit molded by his holy hands.

" . . . God's creative power does not in fact fashion us as though out of soft clay: it is a fire that kindles life in whatever it touches, a quickening spirit . . . " (Teilhard de Chardin)

A quickening spirit! That's when I catch my breath, jump in joy, grasp a new idea, or even when we turn to one another at the bidding of the priest for peace, and I touch you with my fingertips and lips . . . and though we have only moved a little, suddenly we are quickened, charged with life, and we love. So simple a thing. Our bodies have taught us of what we had been only dimly conscious. And then we return to stillness as the liturgy moves on, but it is all different. Movement has awakened us.

Dance as prayer

If prayer is the central core of life, then dance becomes prayer when we are expressing our relationship to God, to others, and to all the world of matter and spirit, through movement originating from our deepest selves—this same central point of worship. The movements of dance-prayer start from our deep center, flow outward like rivulets into the stream of life, and impart life everywhere. So dance can be a part of prayer, just as stillness can be a part of movement and silence can be a part of music. There is one root; all the rest, movement or stillness, silence or sound, is its expression. The closer to the source, the purer the song.

I think Thomas Merton was speaking of this source when, in *Hagia Sophia,* he wrote: "There is in all things an inexhaustible sweetness and purity, a silence that is a fountain of action and of joy. It rises up in wordless gentleness, and flows out to men from the unseen roots of all created being . . . "

Now we can understand when the psalms say to praise the Lord with the dance! It is a dance that wells from our true nature, from persons not cut off from their inner selves. This dance has found different expressions through the ages, and our own culture has its unique contribution to make.

In the past, dances were an integral part of all aspects of life, such as harvesting, fertility, health, marriage, life and death, and the relation of people to all of nature. They were the way cultures expressed their deepest religious understandings. In our own religious tradition, the Israelites had triumphal and gay processions, circle dances and dances of ecstasy, of which King David's must have been a stupendous example (see 2 Samuel 6:12-15). The early church carried on the tradition of the circle dance and developed the idea of the "ring-dance of the angels." Those graced by God participated in this dance. Throughout the Middle Ages there were a wide variety of dances, some even prescribed for bishops! (See E. Louis Backman, *Religious Dances in the Christian Church and in Popular Medicine,* London: Allen & Unwin, 1952, for a full description of dance in the church.) But a living, deep understanding of the religious significance of dance was being lost in the midst of "development," and so our Western civilization gradually relegated dance, a mode of expression so fundamental to human life, to secular activity. The secular world became its only home.

Found and lost . . .

But all good things emerge and are recreated in new ways. And as we are gradually rediscovering the sacredness of all matter (through mystics like Teilhard, from appalled ecologists, from our own sense of deprivation of the sacred in the life we live), we will discover how to dance and pray with purity and meaning and depth in our own Western way.

. . . and found again

This reemergence of sacred dance will take forms that use aspects of folk dancing, square and popular dancing, ballet and modern dance, and it will draw on the advances in psychological understanding for its depth and freedom and individuality. It will no doubt be affected by disciplines from other cultures, with which, for the first time, the average person has a chance to become acquainted—disciplines such as the movement-meditations of Yoga, of T'ai Chi, of Sufism, and of Zen.

We haven't handed down a tradition of sacred movement from

generation to generation, like that of the sacred dance of India, so we must turn to the artists—the dancers in this case—and ask them to plunge into their own depths and draw, from the living spirit that dwells within them, movements that are meaningful for the church. The dance has to be in relation to all the people of God, learning from them what is soul-satisfying and what is really wanted. Vatican II's Constitution on the Church in the Modern World, in the section entitled "Harmony Between Culture and Christian Formation," states very well this relation of the arts to human development. Of specific interest for those concerned with dance and liturgy are these two sentences in paragraph 62: "Let the church also acknowledge new forms of art which are adapted to our age and are in keeping with the characteristics of various nations and regions. Adjusted in their mode of expression and conformed to liturgical requirements, they may be introduced into the sanctuary when they raise the mind to God."

Dance in the sanctuary

I started dancing in church in 1968. I have danced and taught dance-prayers for the Lord, have mercy, Glory to God, offertory processions, responses to readings, the Our Father, meditation after communion, entrance and recessional processions. These dances were created for liturgies for special feast days or occasions like baptisms, and as part of workshops and retreats at high schools and universities, monasteries and convents. The music used has ranged from Bach to Gelineau psalmody, folk music to pieces specially composed for the occasion.

Whenever and wherever there is dancing as part of the specific worship of the church, it must be clearly prayer and not performance, in keeping with the liturgy and setting, and the congregation should be ready for it.

One way of preparing the congregation for dance is to clarify how greatly the church is already involved in the dance through our very rituals. Think of all the various movements of the priest as he presides in a mass, and all the movements prescribed by the church during the year. The priest bows, raises his hands in so many ways to bless, lifts the bread plate and cup, prostrates himself on Good Friday and at ordination. The people respond by kneeling and bowing and standing. There are processions, as on Palm Sunday, and all the movements of the Easter Vigil. Think

4

of all the rhythms that could be described during each liturgy and throughout the year!

The scriptures also speak of movement. Jesus raises his hands to bless, falls with his face to the ground in the garden of Gethsemane, touches those who need healing. The very words "descent" into hell, "ascension" and "resurrection" convey images of movement. The dancer in the church, as a member of the Christian community with a special gift of understanding and loving movement, lifts up by his art and prayer all the movements of everyday life, uniting them to the deepest gestures of the church.

Participation in the gifts

The congregation can participate in the dance-prayer experience as it is expressed by the movements of a solo dancer of fine quality, who can lift up the people's souls to God through beauty in the same way that a solo singer can. Then there is the participation of a small group of nondancers who are willing to learn beforehand a simple movement-prayer, such as the Our Father. And finally there is the general active involvement of all in a simple circle dance, or even just the joining of hands during the final song.

As a dancer I know the special gifts that dance has to offer— gifts we all need for the fullness of life. They are gifts of rhythm with its exuberance and energy, of motion with its full spectrum of dynamics, ranging from softness and delicacy to piercing strength, and of moving shapes, shapes that can sweep through space awakening undying visions. All these comprise the unique language by which dance communicates. Perhaps dance's most important gift to us lies in its ability to unify us and make us whole by uniting our inward life with our outward expression. And this can be done when the simplest gesture is done meaningfully.

What I have experienced is that the very atmosphere created by people dancing together in prayer is conducive to evoking in an easy and joyful way gifts each of us has—gifts that emerge when we are called to look freely and deeply into ourselves and then share our discoveries with others, focused on one another in God: "When you come together, each one has a hymn, a lesson, a revelation, a tongue, or an interpretation." (1 Corinthians 14:26).

We all have gifts, gifts needed by others, gifts which are shaped from how we see and hear and respond to the world that is inside us and around us. Dance expresses these gifts in an all-inclusive way, for its subject is our very selves: our thoughts, dreams, loves, talents as well as our bodies. And dance, when it is a response from the heart to the living God, is also a special gift in itself— a gift of prayer and praise and transformation.

As St. Paul says: "Do you not know that your body is a temple of the Holy Spirit within you, which you have from God? . . . So glorify God in your body" (1 Corinthians 6:19-20).

Many of the dance ideas in this book will be related to the eucharistic liturgy, the seasons of the church year or to special occasions. Others will simply suggest ways of praying and exploring through movement what our faith is all about.

Dancing people, praise the Lord!

Movement Meditations

To everything, turn, turn, turn.
There is a season, turn, turn, turn,
And a time for every purpose under heaven.

"Alongside a river in Australian New Guinea an old man sits and
stares at the water. A tree trunk drifts past; at certain intervals
it rises to the surface and then sinks again, always with the same
motion. The old man reaches for his drum and softly takes up
the rhythm that he has discovered. While he beats the drum, the
image of a dance takes form in his mind." (Described by Gerardus
van der Leeuw in *Sacred and Profane Beauty: the Holy in Art,*
Abingdon Press.)

Repetition and rhythm—part of the very nature of the universe
it seems. No wonder the importance of repetition and rhythm in
our rites. There are the great rhythms of the seasons with their
corresponding festivals, but I am more aware of the smaller
rhythms that make up our rites: the gestures of the presider, the
timing of the handshake, the sign of the cross, the genuflections,
the movement to and from communion, the songs and dances we
use (that have the power to lead us into sleep or meditation, into
agitation or joy).

Our common, everyday rhythm could be described as a walking
tempo. The slower, more sustained rhythms of the rites and
gestures of the liturgy, when done with the consciousness of the
power of their slowness, can by their contrast lead us into the
sacred nature of time.

We need to stamp and hug and use strong rhythms to feel our
feet on the ground and the heartiness and wholeness of life. But
we need to slowly touch, and slowly make sacred signs, to awaken
ourselves to the incredible depth and layers of the universe—to
make a new kind of contact with one another and with the world
of mystery.

Here is a simple exercise you might try that illustrates how playing with time by slowing down an ordinary rhythm can serve to heighten our awareness of one another. It is a kind of handshake.

Take partners. Each person, with extreme slowness, extends the right hand towards the partner's hand. When your hands touch, clasp them and immediately look into the other person's eyes. Hold this a moment, and then move on to somebody else and repeat the same sequence.

This leads me to reflect on the importance of the rhythm of the handshake of peace, or kiss of peace. If the contact with another is hurried, perfunctory, in fact the opposite of the little exercise described, the effect is worse than no gesture at all. (The opposite would be a quick gesture and touch, and an immediate turning of the head away from the person you're greeting.) The head turning away is ostensibly to greet someone else, but what it does is communicate lack of ease—maybe even a wish that the other person didn't exist. I'm not recommending my exercise to replace the hurried kiss of peace, but to do it as a balance to our usual hurriedness and to help free us to establish from within a real communicating rhythm.

The rhythms of the presider in liturgy are of extreme importance. He is called to be an *artist* in his sensitivity to how his inner and outer self draws people into worship. I have seen a priest, while saying "lift up your hearts," raise his arms with such strength and fullness that the hearts of all the congregation were lifted and they raised their arms with him. One needn't be a dancer in order to express through gestures the meaning of the prayer and where one's heart is. We have beautiful, powerful movements within us if we will allow them to come forth. But we can learn from dancers. A dancer will repeat exercises over and over again, always seeking deeper skill and understanding of how to perform the step. If it is a mindless repetition little is learned. But if each time he or she is focusing on some aspect of the movement, gradually a perfection and beauty will emerge.

"Do you not know that your body is a temple of the Holy Spirit . . . ?" (1 Corinthians 6:19). The priest, as artist of this temple, unites himself, body and spirit, and through this union and transparency leads others to a new living relationship with God and with one another. We see each other in holiness. (Also the function of liturgical dancers!)

10

The following is a simple dance-prayer, incorporating rhythms and repetitions, to "Day by Day," choreographed by Charley, Sarah, Greg and Mary Lou at a dance workshop given at the Institute for the Study of Religious Education and Service, Boston College, July 1975. I recommend it particularly for high school and college liturgies or retreats. (Many other versions have been devised—feel free to adapt it to your needs.)

Music from *Godspell*—to be played very slowly:

Day by day. Three people are standing in a circle formation, with hands joined. They come together, lifting their arms up, until they touch in the center.

Day by day. With a slight impulse all move backwards, hands still joined, heads lifted.

O dear Lord. All come together as before, hands lifted together in prayer in the center.

Three things we pray. All kneel, heads bowed, hands assuming individual attitudes of prayer (or none at all—simply dropping by the sides).

To see thee more clearly. All bring their hands toward their eyes and slowly separate them, each turning or lifting his head, as if really seeing in a new way.

Love thee more dearly. All draw their hands to their hearts and then reach out toward one another, palms facing upward, as in an offering.

Follow thee more nearly, day by day . . . All stand, and in a line formation, walk and weave their way toward the other people who are standing or sitting around watching the dance. A few of these are then drawn in and a new, larger circle is formed. The whole sequence is then repeated, each time more and more people being picked up and included during the last refrain. It continues until all are in the dance.

It is simple, but in its ease and repetition is its strength. Sing it and dance it very slowly and it will become a prayer.

Everyone sees beauty in his or her own particular way. This is a description of how to combine everyone's perceptions and create a shared litany of praise. (Fun for all ages, though children, when in a large group of adults, tend to be shy about expressing their images—so be gentle with them.)

A litany of praise

11

Begin with a reflection on the language of dance. There is a silent language all around us—the language of the dance. The words it speaks are movements, movements that reveal their meaning through shapes and directions, degrees of energy and rhythms.

How do we perceive and understand this movement-language of dance? For instance, what dance is happening in a garden?

The leaves of a tree shimmer and are still—momentarily as still as the trunk of the tree.

A fly zigzags with great speed and energy. Another insect ascends at one quarter of the speed—moving as if weightless, dependent on the air, vanishing out of sight.

A slender blade of grass rotates back and forth, back and forth, like an old-fashioned clock, like a mother wagging her finger.

A little ant moves in his rapid way of always seeming to know where he is going.

A chunky bird's wings fuss and flutter as he hops from low leaves to grass, pecking at the earth. In his natural movement there is a speed that is like that of an electric drill, the simple hopping rhythm of a child, as well as the sublime capacity to soar.

Suddenly we see a hummingbird with his near-invisible wings, and a plane drones overhead!

"The fish in the water is silent, the animal on the earth is noisy, and the bird in the air is singing. But man has in him the silence of the sea, the noise of the earth and the music of the air." (Rabindranath Tagore)

"All thy works shall give thanks to thee, O Lord" (Psalm 145).

"We are not alone in our acts of praise. Whenever there is life, there is silent worship. The world is always on the verge of becoming one in adoration. It is man who is the cantor of the universe, and in whose life the secret of cosmic prayer is disclosed." (Abraham Heschel)

After this introductory reflection, invite everyone to close their eyes and think of one or two things they have seen lately, or felt, whose force of beauty has really struck them. For example, it could be bands of color in the sky, or a little child playing in the waves. Make a phrase of it like this: "Children playing in the waves, praise the Lord!" or "Mountains and sky, praise the Lord!" Now think of how the image might be conveyed through movement and combine the words and movement.

When everyone is ready, form a circle. One person starts, speaks and dances his image as the rest watch, and then all repeat after him his words and actions. The next person in the circle will then do the same—dance and speak a new line of praise and then all repeat it. Continue around the circle in the same manner.

As this is a beginning dance-prayer experience, the movements should be simple, almost pictorial. (For example, let's use the line "Falling leaves, praise the Lord!" The leader might move his or her hands gently toward the floor, in uneven rhythms, as leaves move that are tossed about when blown in the wind. "Praise the Lord!" could be danced as part of that downward movement, or with hands lifted upward, as if they were leaves flung high, or there could be a uniform gesture of upraised arms that would be done after everyone's phrase.) Ending each phrase with "Praise the Lord!" establishes a rhythm and form that creates a feeling of security and allows the first part of the line to be original and personal.

When everyone in the circle has shared a phrase, end with a song of praise, or a uniform gesture to a line from a psalm, such as: "Let everything that breathes praise the Lord" (Psalm 150). (All could circle around themselves, arms outstretched.)

Hands and prayer

A meditation—hands and prayer: Close your eyes. Stand very still, arms at your sides, feet slightly apart. Be aware of your breath— the in and out, in and out. All of life is in motion, yet there is "the still point." Find that still point within you. It is from there that your movements will come. It is from your still point that your movements will be a dialogue with God—your heart united with his; your hands moving, talking, in his space. Feel the presence of God in the space around you.

"I will lift up my hands and call on thy name" (Psalm 63). Slowly lift your hands in a wordless dialogue with God.

"Then he led them out as far as Bethany, and lifting up his hands, he blessed them" (Luke 24:50). Lift your hands again, with your palms facing upward. After they are lifted, slowly turn your palms face downward and lower your arms. Pretend you are blessing someone, placing your hands on her head. How do your hands feel? Do you sense warmth and a kind of gentle energy in them?

13

Bring your right hand toward your heart and slightly bend over, rounding your upper body. Now move your hand up and out, straightening your torso at the same time, wordlessly offering your self to God. Repeat the gesture: in to the heart and out, in and out, moving a little faster each time, until you are joyfully extending yourself. (Jump in the air on the last offering if you wish to.)

"Let my prayer be counted as incense before thee, and the lifting of my hands as an evening sacrifice!" (Psalm 141). Incense slowly turns and twists as it curls upward. Lift your hands upward as if they were one column of incense, and create a flowing, turning, moving prayer. Stop when your hands are at a comfortable height. Feel the stillness, the shape of your hands.

Stretch your arms far out to the sides. Hold them so, not stiffly, and feel the energy going out and out and out. Now curve them slightly, rounding them, as if to embrace the whole world, or, more simply, as if you were embracing a group of children in front of you.

Psalm 103

Bless the Lord, O my soul;
And all that is within me, bless his holy name!

Find a still, private spot. For a special sense of peace and beauty, place a candle in front of you. Kneel and sit back on your heels. Lengthen your spine, rest your hands on your knees, and close your eyes. Just be still and peaceful, breathing easily.

Slowly say the first line to yourself and bring your hands to a prayer position in front of your chest, with palms together, fingers pointed up.

With your own rhythm and altering your hands so that they feel right to you, raise your arms straight up, lifting your back and head as you do so, as if all that is within you is being drawn upward from the very center of your being.

On the words "bless his holy name," bend your body all the way forward and lower your arms to the floor in front of you. Hold for a moment.

Now come back to your starting position, hands on knees, back straight.

Repeat this movement sequence several times till it becomes your own.

It is not too big a step for you to now call forth from yourself your own movements to this, or to another line from scripture.

With the right preparation and setting (such as a liturgy for a small group or a prayer-service), this type of danced prayer can be used, for instance, as a responsorial with the psalm of the day. Arrange all who will participate in a circle and teach the movements. The dancers move as the responsorial line is read, and sit in stillness for the rest of the psalm.

A dance-meditation for a small group (based on the line from Psalm 19, "Let the words of my mouth and the meditation of my heart be acceptable in thy sight, O Lord . . . "):

Let the words of my mouth . . .

Though this phrase suggests a meditation danced by one person, here is a way of doing it for a group of three, four or five people. The group forms a circle. Each person in the group takes an opening position at a different level, in a sequential order, that is, the first person is very low, crouched over; the second person is a little higher; the third person is kneeling; the fourth is in a low standing position, and the fifth is fully standing. Every person now assumes a body position related to the prayer (hands to mouth, or heart, etc.) while maintaining his or her level.

Now we begin to "pass the prayer." All hold still in their poses while the first person improvises, moving her hands, head, torso, staying in touch with whatever feeling is working out from the inside. She maintains her low position as she moves and repeats softly the words to herself ("Let the words of my mouth and the meditation of my heart be acceptable in thy sight, O Lord"). She finishes the movements by turning to the person next to her. With her hands, she "offers the prayer" and then holds this offering position.

The second person "takes" the prayer with a gesture and then continues with his own improvisation, maintaining his slightly raised level, and in turn offers his prayer to the third person, holding his final position. All continue in like manner.

The final person, who is standing the most upright, taking all these prayers, adds his own and "lifts them all up" by raising his hands to God in whatever way that comes from within. He then becomes absolutely still, and all hold their final prayer position for a few more seconds.

15

I have found this prayer-movement sequence to be very simple but effective. A number of people might practice and try it as a prayer before the gospel. (How I would love to see the presider as the final person in the circle.) When I have groups try it in workshops I use meditative music in the background. The dance-prayer form originated as a result of prayer and need. I was searching for an idea of how to choreograph these lines for the Omega Dance Group in New York City when we were to do them as part of a Sabbath service, and the image came. Eight of us formed a wide semicircle and improvised in exactly the above form, while the cantor slowly chanted the line. It was the simplest but most valid dance-prayer we performed in the service.

These suggestions, emphasizing hand movements, are all solemn. But hands can clap, press, kiss. As it says in Isaiah 55:12, "and all the trees of the field shall clap their hands." Create exuberant hand dances, too!

Meditation and dance

All persons active in ministry—including dancers—need times of withdrawal in order to center themselves and refresh their spirits. The following method of meditation leading to movement was written for this book by Arthur Eaton, Jr., psychotherapist and program coordinator of the Omega Liturgical Dance Company.

When a person attains a quiet and unhindered relationship to God (or his Spirit), there occurs an inflow of inspiration which later may be expressed through an art form. Our interest is in how this inspiration can give dance an unexpected and fresh quality.

Dance, in a general sense, refers to all movements, whether vegetative, human, planetary or celestial. Human dance has many forms and styles, but liturgical or sacred dance refers to movement made through and in relation to the Spirit of God. This may include everything from simple head or hand movements, tapping of the feet, choreographed sacred or liturgical dance, to spontaneous movements of the body arising from at-one-ness with the source of inspiration.

Christian meditation involves an attentive but quiet state of receptiveness in which the basic objective is to attain communion with God. Meditation in this sense serves as a mediating process.

When a silent meditator succeeds in disengaging from customary attention to body, feelings and mental activities, the intuition can sense new inspirations. These may be experienced in the form of visualized symbols, inner hearing, subtle impressions leading to new awareness, or simply as flows of energy and light.

When meditation precedes a dance, its purpose is to make an individual available to God. In a quiet state, inspiration can enter and release a flow of movement whose sources are richly watered by the Spirit. Such movements are not necessarily derived from learned technique and are both harmonious and exciting. They are a physical expression of the spiritual message received during meditation. They may come spontaneously at the time, or they may be choreographed later.

Training in meditation includes methods for observing and quieting the body and disciplines to develop focused attention to inner psychic processes relating to the feelings and the mind. These improve sensitivity to the passage of subtle energies and impressions from Spirit. Practices may include creative use of visualization and the imagination. These in turn lead to the highest form of meditation called contemplation in which one becomes fully receptive to God. Valuable suggestions may be found in the writings of Ramacharaka, a Westerner deeply trained in Christianity and the Eastern tradition of meditation. His book *Raja Yoga* (on the yoga of the mind) is highly recommended.

Our experience with meditation in relation to dance leads us to make the following recommendations:

1. Take a comfortable seated position in a straight back chair. For the more agile, a cross-legged position sitting on a cushion or the floor can be taken.

2. Within a Christian frame of reference, preface the meditation by a brief prayer establishing a personal relationship with God.

3. Disengage from any internal or external distractions while mentally affirming the intent to quiet the body, mind and feelings. When distractions arise, simply allow them to pass by, objectively observing them but recognizing their separateness from your center point of stillness.

4. Consciously call upon God to empty and purify the personality so as to better serve him.

5. Take a few moments to observe and attune to the flow of the breath.

Focus concentrated attention upon one of the following: the heart, a point just in front of the forehead, or the name of Jesus. Keep coming back to the focus chosen when other thoughts, memories or concerns intrude into consciousness.

7. In silence, identify the objective of the meditation. Is it to seek help, such as clarifying or resolving a problem? Is it to receive guidance to carry out some spiritual purpose? Or is it simply to be open to new inspiration, in this instance, for dance?

8. Just prior to going into silence, it may be found to be helpful to use visualization and creative imagination to see the self in rapport with God's Spirit. This may be done by silent adoration, or picturing the Christ-light filling and flooding the entire person.

Each individual is free to develop his or her particular method of preparation for entering the silence. However, upon completion of these preparatory steps enter a state of focused, attentive and receptive silence for from five to ten minutes. As a sense of joy and peace enter, allow a state of just *being* to continue for a while.

Upon completion of the predetermined time for meditation, slowly unwind, gradually becoming more conscious of the body. With gentle movements, as though guided by an inner breath, allow the limbs, head and torso to express something of what was experienced in meditation. Let these movements develop spontaneously and note that they seem to be inspired by something independent of usual thought processes, yet they can be observed while quiet and centered. Such self-observation should in no way pull one from the inner centeredness which is at the core of the movement. While moving from silence into movement, slowly uncurl the fingers, unfold the spine and stretch the extremities. Let this process be experienced as if inside a plant, perhaps opening as a rose. Feel through this in a combination of detachment, delicacy and gentleness. There may be occasions when the energy released after meditation is far from gentle: explosive, affirmative and definite in expression of will or action, as in Aikido or Bondo. At other times it may be easy and flowing as in Tai Chi. Whatever manifests, it is crucial to be aware of the still point in the center of God's light.

> . . . and the wind came, and the man/woman plant
> unfolded, stretched, turned and danced.

> *—Brian Eaton*

Dance and the Eucharist

In this chapter, I will offer some suggestions for the ordinary parts of the eucharistic liturgy—both for congregational movement and for small group dances.

Artists may have a special role to play in the church, but congregations have more to contribute than they realize. Dancers must test out their own movements (do they really help the congregation to pray?) and find movements that all people can use and be enriched by. Otherwise the dancer ends up praying alone before a congregation of spectators.

Movement is of little value in worship if it is too complicated, or if it becomes mechanical, or if it is "performed" rather than assimilated and made the person's own. I wonder if the movements prescribed for the priest and for the congregation at worship were ever taught in ways that brought out their real values. For the worshiper seeking to understand gesture and prayer, it is important to understand these three points:

1. Doing a movement correctly is not as important as allowing your soul to fill the movement.

2. Getting the various *positions* right isn't the most important thing. How a person moves from one position to another, how one fills out the path between, is the greater part of the dance. (When a person jumps from one pose to another it is like a singer's jumping, staccato, from one salient note to the next, never sustaining a phrase, never noticing the notes between on the score.)

3. How you look isn't important; what's important is how you feel (as if God were feeling your prayer, not looking at your movements).

When you practice the following directions, notice words like *slowly, sustained, continuous,* and allow your own inner prayer to direct and mold your body. Feel free to alter the movements so as to develop a natural feeling with danced prayer. We find the movements work best when they are done *really* slowly.

Welcoming the Sabbath

"Sanctify the Sabbath by choice meals, by beautiful garments; delight your soul with pleasure and I will reward you for this very pleasure." —Abraham Heschel, *The Sabbath*

Dancing is like a beautiful garment, a garment in which the spirit moves and delights and in which it can reach out and greet the Sabbath, the Lord's Day. When we dance we can recognize our own beauty (if we let ourselves be simple) and with all creation simply be, thus spontaneously praising the Lord. To dance is to know we are chosen, chosen creatures, responding with a human soul to God's chosen time. Abraham Heschel writes, " . . . on the Sabbath we try to become attuned to holiness in time"; it is a day "to turn from the results of creation to the mystery of creation." Let us take time and dance from the inside, slowly, and welcome the Sabbath by making new the way we enter a special dwelling—the dwelling where we celebrate and worship every week. By taking time, moving in special ways, we perceive a presence—the presence of the Sabbath.

The following "greeting" dance is a lovely way to welcome and to usher into the church building all the people coming to worship in a Sunday eucharist.

Three people (priest, deacon, and a lay person) stand inside the doors; the congregation waits outside (or dances outside—see second suggestion). When the doors open each person goes to one of the three, holding arms out, about waist level, palms turned upward. The greeter (palms turned downward) touches the other's palms (or in any way that seems natural, warm and gentle). I found that as one of the "greeters," I was not only blessing the person with my palms, but bowing slightly. This is followed with a slight gesture that shows the direction to move when entering (to the right, left, etc.). The effect is to say without words, and with quiet love, "This is a special place—you are specially welcome."

This could be done in silence or with music sung or played by a soloist, chorus, or everybody. The movement suggests deep joy and also the rest of the Sabbath. With music, the movement is tied to the mood and rhythm of the piece, not the words, and the song can be repeated over and over again.

After being welcomed, in the way described, the people slowly move around (hopefully there is space in the back of the church) weaving from one person to the next, greeting one another with the left hand, as in an informal "grand-right-and-left" of square dancing. When all are inside the building and the greeting dance has gone on long enough, the people file slowly down the aisle to the pews or sanctuary, lifting up their arms, turning, singing, depending on their openness and ease.

The second suggestion is for the congregation to be doing a simple circle or processional dance outside the church building. This can be done by just joining hands and walking slowly in time to the music. The leader would eventually break the circle and lead everybody, as in a snake dance, to the doors. The music would be played continuously until all are greeted, ushered in and are in their usual places for the service.

Carey Landry's "Hymn of Praise" (from his album, *I Will Never Forget You,* published by North American Liturgy Resources) was choreographed by Sister Dorin Sayonne, under my direction, as part of her work at the Institute for the Study of Religious Education and Service at Boston College. It is suitable as an entrance rite (as described here) or for the Glory to God. It was first performed at a mass attended by about two hundred students. I was deeply impressed by the effect it had on the whole liturgy. The gestures were of the utmost simplicity, yet the "Hymn of Praise" set a tone of awe and reverence that lasted throughout the mass.

The altar was placed in the middle of the congregation, with chairs grouped so that six aisles were made in a star-like formation. Previously the chairs had been set up in straight rows, so this was the first time the members of the congregation were facing one another. Some people didn't even notice the dancers kneeling at the back of their own aisle, on the floor right next to them. But they could see those in the aisles facing them, gathered in small groups directed toward the altar. As the hymn was sung, the dancers gradually moved toward the altar, with steady and then more flowing movements, until they circled it in the formation described below. After a final bow all the dancers remained in a low kneeling position as two priests, who were part of the dance, stood up and began the blessing and sprinkling of water. Taking branches they had picked, they dipped them in bowls of water on the altar and ceremoniously moved around

"Hymn of Praise"

blessing everyone while saying prayers. This led right into the Lord, have mercy.

The dancers mentioned above were students who had attended the dance and prayer workshop of the Institute and who had, for the most part, never danced before. Nevertheless, through the use of space and rhythm and gesture they were able to lift everyone in the congregation to a heightened sense of the presence of God.

Note: The three-line refrain with corresponding gestures used throughout the danced "Hymn of Praise" ("We praise you"/arms lifted, "We bless you"/arms crossed over chest, "We worship you"/bow) was sung and performed twice by the congregation for the memorial acclamation. It gave an unusually good sense of unity to the liturgy.

The dance is done in groups of five or six people.

We praise you. Kneeling on your heels with your head touching the floor, gradually raise your body from the waist up to a kneeling position. At the same time, slowly raise your hands in front of you in a gesture of offering and praise.

We bless you. Lower your body back on your heels and cross your arms on your chest.

We worship you. In the above position, lower your body from the waist down until your head touches the floor. Extend your arms in front of you with palms down.

We praise you. Gradually come up from the above position to a kneeling position. Bring your left leg up and raise yourself to a standing position, gradually raising your hands in front of you in a gesture of praise, and take one step forward.

We bless you. While standing in place cross your arms on your chest.

We worship you. Bring your right leg behind you and bend on one knee to a kneeling position with your arms at your side, palms facing forward.

We praise you. Raise yourself to a standing position and, while walking, raise your hands in a slightly higher gesture of praise.

We bless you. Continue walking and cross your arms on your chest.

We worship you. Bring your right leg behind you and bend on one knee to a kneeling position with your arms at your side, palms facing forward (same as above).

Here each group works in two sets of two or three people:

For you alone are the holy one. The first set goes forward toward the altar, repeating the gesture of praise with arms raised above the head, while the second set holds the previous position until the next line.

You alone are the Lord. The first set backs away and bends right legs to a kneeling position, with arms at the side and palms facing forward, as the second set moves toward the altar, raising arms in praise.

You alone are the most high. The first set moves toward the altar in a gesture of praise while the second set backs away to a kneeling position.

Jesus Christ. The first set holds the position of arms raised over the head; the second set comes forward with arms raised over the head and forms a second circle behind the first set.

Jesus Christ. Still in two circles with arms raised over the head, all look up.

We praise you. Still in two circles with one moving to the right and the other the left, walk with hands extended in front, repeating the first gesture of praise.

We bless you. Still walking in a circle, cross your arms on your chest.

We worship you. Face altar. Bend your right leg behind you and bend one knee to a kneeling position, with your arms at your side, palms facing forward.

Here are two congregational gestures designed for a traditional alleluia in the Gregorian style—three times chanted by the cantor, three times repeated by the congregation.

The gospel alleluia

1. As the cantor begins, a member of the congregation takes the lectionary and walks slowly to the presider, moving in time with the chant. The congregation stands. On the response, the presider raises the book while the members of the congregation chant and ready themselves to receive the word of God through the following movement sequence: first they bow and slowly bring their hands to their *hearts,* fingertips pointing inward, then slowly up to their *mouths* (while straightening their backs), then to their *foreheads,* and finish by opening their arms sideways (with a slight impulse) as if having been cleansed. (The movement of the back is important. It starts bent slightly forward and

rounded and then slowly uncurls until, on the last gesture, it is as open and lifted as possible without strain). All the movements are done as one continuous fluid gesture, timed so they flow with the three alleluias. At the end, in silence, the arms are lowered and all stand very still, now ready to listen.

2. As the cantor sings, slowly lift up your head and move one arm upward at the same time, in a sustained, light and slow way. Draw the back of your hand toward your face. On the second alleluia, lift the other arm in a similar manner, as if the hand were searching for the first one. On the third alleluia, the hands move upward together, separating at the peak, palms facing outward. From the first alleluia onward sustain, and even increase, the up and backward arch of the back. For the response, just lower your arms, slowly finishing with the chant. (*A gentle, lovely suggestion by Janet Periolat.*)

Holy, holy

A group of us have fallen naturally into doing the following movements during the introductory dialogue of the preface:

> *Lift up your hearts.* The presider raises his arms, looking up.
>
> *We lift them up to the Lord.* All raise their arms, looking up.
>
> *Let us give thanks to the Lord our God.* All hold the above gesture while the presider bows.
>
> *It is right to give him thanks and praise.* All bow, lowering arms.

Holy, holy, holy Lord. Cup hands together, palms in front of face, and bend your body slightly forward. Close your eyes—it will help you feel this gesture of awe before God.

God of power and might. Bow deeply, lowering arms.

heaven and earth are full of your glory. Make a full circle with your arms by crossing them in front of your body, lifting them up and, with an impulse, opening them wide to the sides and then lowering them. This is done as one movement, with a feeling of fullness and openness. It will flow into the next gesture.

Hosanna in the highest. Bend your knees slightly. Then straighten them, at the same time swinging your arms up in front of you with a feeling of praise.

Blessed is he who comes in the name of the Lord. Fold your arms across your chest while bowing slightly, and then open them, taking the hand of the person on either side of you.

Hosanna in the highest. Holding hands, raise your arms as in the first "hosanna."

Let there be light!

Abraham Heschel writes in *The Sabbath*, "When all work is brought to a standstill, the candles are lit. Just as creation began with a word, 'Let there be light!' so does the celebration of creation begin with the kindling of lights. It is the woman who ushers in the joy, and sets up the most exquisite symbol, light, to dominate the atmosphere of the home."

Wouldn't it be lovely if at the time of the sanctus, to emphasize the holiness of all creation, candles were brought to the altar? Why not have a number of women, perhaps one from each family if the congregation is small, as well as single women, come forward with candles (they could be distributed during the preparation of the gifts), light them from a central candle, and slowly circle the altar as the preface and sanctus are sung or chanted. At the end all could pause, lift their candles high, place them on the altar or, preferably, around it (sand makes an excellent candle holder), and deeply bow (not with a feeling of uniformity, but with slowness and dignity) and return to their places.

Another way would be for the women to bring up the candles during the preface and, placing them down, dance the Holy, holy as described above. It would be beautiful if the presider also joined in the dance. If not, he should simply raise his arms with a gesture of blessing, experiencing the mystery of his uplifted hands in a holy place, responding to God's presence.

All this simple movement should be done with the consciousness of being within a presence. Rabbi Heschel says we are within the Sabbath, not the Sabbath within us. Any music that is chosen should also contribute to this special sense.

A

The memorial acclamations

Christ has died. Bend over and cross your arms in front of your body, with a feeling of sorrow and burden. Allow your knees to bend.

Christ is risen. In one movement straighten your knees, drop your arms, lift your body and raise your arms sideways and upward in a circular motion. Have a sense of opening and stretching your whole body. (You may have to open your arms in back of the person standing next to you.)

Christ will come again. Continue the circular movement of the arms upward, cross them in front of your body and clasp the hands of the person on either side. *(Suggested by Ted Welch—to be done with power and affirmation.)*

Note: If using Joe Wise's version ("Christ has died, alleluia; Christ is risen, alleluia; Christ will come again, alleluia"), on "Christ will come again" circle in place to the right with a joyful feeling. Repeat.

B

Dying you destroyed our death. From a kneeling position, slowly move your head in a complete circle (drop it forward, reach toward the right shoulder, continue to the back, to the left shoulder and down to the chest again) with a sense of mourning, or sorrow, as in a pieta.

rising you restored our life. Slowly come to standing. Keep your weight forward, toward the balls of the feet. Feel very lifted, expectant.

Lord Jesus, come in glory. Extend your arms softly outward, palms facing upward. Allow your hands to rest over or under someone else's in a supporting manner. *(Suggested by Kateri Terns—to be done with simplicity.)*

C

When we eat this bread and drink this cup. Cup your hands in front of you like a chalice (as if they contained all that the Lord's body and blood mean to you) and slowly raise your hands upward in this position. Follow your hands with your eyes, letting your head also lift upward.

we proclaim your death, Lord Jesus, until you come in glory. Open your hands and fingers with a slight impulse, and then extend them very slowly sideways. This is done with a quiet feeling of radiating the good news. Keep your arms lowering until the final moment. You can imagine the Lord's mercies and gifts showering down on us. Try this as a movement in canon when singing the music as a round. *(This is mine.)*

D

Lord, by your cross and resurrection you have set us free. Start with your arms crossed against your chest, hands clasped to shoulders, head lowered. Feel the weight of your arms. Slowly raise your elbows up, then your head, unclasp your hands from your shoulders and stretch your arms up and outward, ending on the word "free." Pause for a second in this position. Enjoy the feeling of moving from the stricture of the cross to the freedom of the stretch.

You are the Savior of the world. Slowly lower your arms to the sides in a full arc, bending the knees slightly. Draw your hands together in front of your body while straightening the knees, palms facing upwards, as if you are holding the world in your hands. *(Suggested by Nick Hodsdon.)*

"Keep in Mind" (from *Biblical Hymns and Psalms* by Lucien Deiss, World Library Publications, Inc.) is often used as an alternative memorial acclamation. I have begun introducing the movements below to accompany the antiphon. I have done this only at college and special retreat liturgies. You will note that the movements require an open space, instead of the usual pews.

From "Keep in mind" through "saving Lord" all slowly move around, touching first the right hand of one person then the left hand of the next, and so on (as in a grand right and left, but with no formal circle or order). This is done prayerfully, meeting the eyes of the other person, singing or saying silently with hands, eyes and hearts, "Keep in mind," "Jesus has died for us," "is risen from the dead," "he is our saving Lord," etc.

On "he is joy for all ages," all raise arms and slowly turn in place, heads and hearts lifted joyfully.

Pause during the refrain and repeat the same movements each time the antiphon is sung.

Note: The mood of the entire liturgy should be deeply reverent, special and personal. The walking and passing hand gesture then fits in beautifully, adding to the acclamation a moment of prayerful human contact, sheltered in the presence of the divine.

This is very simple. All join hands, including (and especially) with

"Keep in Mind"

The great amen

those across the aisle (the people at the end of the pews will have to move into the aisle to do this), and raise your arms. Feel your whole being assent to the AMEN.

The Lord's Prayer

It is possible for a dance to the Lord's Prayer to be simple enough for a whole congregation to learn with as much practice as they would normally have for a song (around five minutes). To do this well, the leader should have assimilated the movements beforehand, so that he or she can teach them in a flowing way, and be able to put his or her own soul into the prayer without self-consciousness.

Here is a simple version of an Our Father dance. I have taught this more than any other group dance—to children and adults, sitting or standing, in groups of all sizes. It is always so moving to see a whole group of worshipers bowing and raising arms in praise!

The text used here is the one prepared in 1975 by the International Consultation on English Texts.

Opening position: Cross your arms in front of your body and take the hands of the person on either side of you. Still holding hands, bend over and remain in this position for a moment, with a sense of stillness and prayer.

Our Father in heaven, hallowed be your Name; your kingdom come, your will be done, on earth as in heaven. Slowly raise your torso and at the same time lift your arms up in a smooth, continuous way, holding your neighbors' hands until you naturally let them go as your arms lift higher. (Avoid any pulling.) Uncross your arms (there will be a lovely moment of expansion when everyone does this at the same time) and hold them in an open, praising position, head and chest upraised.

Give us today our daily bread. Lower your arms, bringing your hands together in a gesture of petition (palms face upward, arms stretched out in front of you about chest height).

Forgive us our sins. Bow forward folding your arms to your chest with a sense of contrition.

as we forgive those who sin against us. Come out of the bow and take the hands of the person on either side of you as a gesture of reconciliation. (Do not cross your arms this time.)

Save us from the time of trial. Holding hands, all bow deeply.

And deliver us from evil. Hold bow.

Priest: "Deliver us, Lord, from every evil . . . "

For the kingdom, the power, and the glory are yours, now and forever. Amen. All raise arms and torsos, hands still joined. Rise to toes, and letting go of neighbors' hands, raise hands even higher in an exuberant amen!

From a dancer's point of view the congregational kiss of peace was the most spirit-releasing change introduced into the mass. It requires that people *move,* and move in a context of love for one another. As a dancer, my body is dulled during a long mass with no physical expression, and then someone reaches toward me, smiles, touches my hand, or cheek, and my spirit *leaps*—leaps because my whole being is suddenly involved.

    Though there have been mixed reactions to the introduction of the congregational kiss of peace, I think most people welcomed it. The familiar way of greeting is probably the best for most occasions. It allows a person's spontaneity to come out, and that is most important. However, I'm going to describe here three more stylized variations of the usual, natural way of greeting. These are useful in liturgies that have special significance, or that call for a more ritualized approach. Conversely, if a liturgy already has much dance in it, my experience suggests it is better to keep the kiss of peace absolutely natural, to balance the more choreographed parts.

The kiss of peace

I have taught the following dance expression of the kiss of peace widely to many varying groups. It was done to conclude the final leave-taking rite at the 1975 Liturgical Week held in Princeton, New Jersey. It is set to the Israeli folk song "Shalom Chaverim," or "Shalom, My Friends."

"Shalom, My Friends"

> Shalom, my friends,
> Shalom, my friends,
> Shalom, shalom.
> May peace be with you, ('til we meet again)
> May peace be with you, ('til we meet again)
> Shalom, shalom.

In a small group, the dance can be done with everybody in a set formation of two concentric circles. In a large group, people can just mill around, finding partners at random. The basic pattern is as follows:

Shalom, my friends, Shalom, my friends. Each participant walks toward a partner; they greet one another in a friendly manner with their eyes, arms held slightly lifted to the sides.

Shalom, shalom. By this third "shalom" all should be facing a partner, standing about a foot apart. Bringing hands together in the traditional prayer position (palms together, fingertips pointing upward), each bows to the other. (In Hindu tradition, when you bow to another you bow to God present within the person. I have found that most people find this a helpful insight.) The torso is straightened, keeping hands together, as the shalom is repeated.

May peace be with you. All extend and clasp right hands with partner.

May peace be with you. Keeping right hands clasped, left hand is extended (crossing over right hands) and clasps partner's left hand.

Shalom. Keeping hands crossed and clasped, partners raise arms while stepping toward one another, rising to the balls of their feet. This is done with a graceful dip and upward curve as partners come together.

Shalom. Taking a step away from each other, arms and torsos are lowered, with hands still clasped, as partners bow to one another, then part. As the song repeats, all begin walking toward a new partner.

Note: The refrain should be repeated at least seven or eight times, allowing the people to really learn the pattern and to enter deeply into the ritual with a number of partners. To teach the dance, demonstrate with one other person, asking him or her to mirror your movements. Mention to all that the dance can be done in groups of three as well as in pairs, so that nobody need be left out.

If the group is composed of about twenty people and you would like the kiss of peace to be done more formally, ask all to form two concentric circles (one inside the other). Make sure each circle has the same number of people. The inside circle faces outward, backs to the center, and remains in that position. The outside circle will move clockwise, advancing one person each time the song is repeated, moving on "Shalom, my friends, shalom, my friends."

Following are two movement versions of the kiss of peace composed by Danielle Bonetti and Michael Reiling, students in my dance workshop at the Institute for the Study of Religious Education and Service held at Boston College in the summer of 1976. The first was composed with folk masses in mind, and the second version for solemn liturgies.

In the folk version, all walk toward a partner, stop, and, facing one another, extend right hands from the heart toward the other. Hands clasp. They immediately unclasp and are placed on the right shoulder of the partner. Partners walk around in a circle (clockwise), holding this position. All break and move on to another partner.

Note: We did this in silence, but I can imagine the movements done to a joyous musical background.

The formal version incorporates the idea of bowing to God's presence in one another, as in the "Shalom, My Friends" described above. When it was done during a liturgy at Boston College, two priests who concelebrated demonstrated the gestures with one another first, and then asked everyone to do likewise. What followed were a few minutes filled with reverence and dignity.

Directions: Two people face one another. One person bows with hands held in prayer position (palms together, fingertips pointing upward) as a sign of reverence for the other. Then the same person straightens up and places his or her hands on the head of the other person in a gesture of blessing. After a slight pause the same gestures (first bowing and then blessing) are done by the second person to the first. Both then separate, turn toward someone else, and repeat the gestures.

Two simple gesture-dances

I hope these suggestions of movement-prayers are helpful. Remember that a congregation will need time to try these movements before the liturgy. It will take a little time for people to assimilate the movements and to feel comfortable with them, before real prayer can flow. With a little willingness, more will be gained than simply "dancing in church."

Real prayer takes time

Seasonal Dances

ADVENT

Ask a dancer to dance non-stop for four weeks! Impossible! Yet
the church easily dances for four weeks. It is only part of her
fifty-two-week dance.

Advent is one of her four-week dances. The themes of this
dance are very rich and mysterious. They include darkness turning
into light, waiting turning into joy, the light within us growing—
symbolized each week by the lighting of first one candle, then
two, then three, and finally all four candles of Advent. The dance,
so to speak, evolves from a solo (one small light standing alone),
to a duet (two lights are joined), to a trio (the energy circulates
and builds), to a quartet that lays the cornerstone for the birth
of something new.

We need to participate in specific dances and rituals that will
bring out for us the deep experiences and meanings of Advent—
dances and dramas that focus on the advent attitudes of needing,
waiting, longing, fearing the darkness of winter yet hoping in and
nurturing the light of Christ within our souls. The hope of this
light longs to be offered as a gift and so be released to grow, even
as it waits to be kindled. It is the recognition and bringing to
light of these movements, stored within our bodies and souls, that
causes them to develop and us to grow as religious persons. We
become more alive in our faith and more aware of who we really
are as a people when together we dance these mysteries. The
seasons become life-giving, rich and full.

The following are dance-prayers for the whole congregation,
followed by dances to be performed by smaller groups within
the congregation, and finally dances and prayer ideas for people
to do in their homes, with their families or communities.

On the First Sunday of Advent (cycle B of the Roman Lectionary)
we read, "Lord, make us turn to you, let us see your face and we

**Lord, make us
turn to you**

35

shall be saved" (Psalm 80). I suggest that the whole congregation pray this response in the following way:

Lord, make us turn to you. Standing, each person, with bowed head, clasps hands together in front of the face.

Let us see your face and we shall be saved. All unclasp their hands and, with palms facing, slowly open their hands sideways (as if parting a curtain), while lifting their heads.

This movement-prayer will be felt even more deeply if the eyes are closed during the first part and opened as the hands are separating. (For all congregational prayer-dances it helps to have a dance leader demonstrate the movement first and then perform the gestures with everybody.)

Maranatha!

Another expression of longing is contained in the beautiful word "Maranatha!" Come, Lord! Following the setting by Lucien Deiss (found in *Biblical Hymns and Psalms,* Vol. I, World Library Publications, Inc.), I suggest that on each refrain the people lift up their heads on the word "Maranatha!" and on "Come, O Christ the Lord!" reach forward with one hand, filling that gesture with their own feeling of longing. The hand is then slowly lowered as the verse is sung, and lifts and reaches forward once again on each refrain.

(Try this exercise first before leading the congregation: Hold your hand in front of you with palm facing up. Sense the passive, waiting feeling that this position conveys. Now *really* reach out with the same hand, letting even your back be drawn forward. Sense the increased feeling of longing that can be experienced and conveyed by this movement.)

Let the clouds . . .

Yet another movement-prayer can be done to the antiphon given in the *Roman Missal* for the Fourth Sunday of Advent (Isaiah 45:8). This could be danced, as described below, while the words are sung or recited, with flute improvisation or guitar used for additional accompaniment. (Once again, see Lucien Deiss's *Biblical Hymns and Psalms,* Vol. I, for a possible setting.)

Let the clouds rain down the Just One. (Stand and feel your feet rooted to the ground, and your spine long—reaching upward and downward at the same time.) Start with your hands held slightly below your chest level. Your palms are open and facing outward, right fingertips pointing upward, left fingertips downward, heels barely touching. As the words begin, slowly separate your hands, moving them in a straight line, in the direction the fingers are pointing, until your right hand is stretched straight overhead and your left hand stretched straight downward. Palms are still facing out.

and the earth bring forth a Savior. Slowly and simultaneously, with a wide arc, stretch your right arm out to the right side and your left arm out to the left side. (You will have drawn, so to speak, the vertical and horizontal arms of the cross, and through the slow, stretching, wide arcing movements, experience a sense of heaven and earth being united.) Hold the final position for a moment, slowly bringing the prayer to a close.

The texts for the three prayers just described have been prayed by the church for centuries. Here is a modern prayer, touching on the advent theme of darkness and light, that emerged from the soul of a friend of mine, Joan Englander. I feel drawn to include it in the hope that a dancer somewhere, in some congregation, will be inspired by it to create a lovely solo dance and offer it as a meditation.

A modern prayer

> Oh Lord God listen to me
> I seek to hear Your calling
> Let the dark spark seek
> its counterpart in light
> unite us with our shadows
> and uplift us beyond
> this blade of darkness.

On the Fourth Sunday of Advent (cycle B of the Roman Lectionary) we read the story of the annunciation (Luke 1:26-38). I see the purpose of the inclusion of this account being not only to lead us into the story of the birth of Christ, but also as a reminder of the purity of heart, willingness to believe, waiting and longing spirit that we all need in order to believe that we are each a bearer of inner light, that our light can greet Christ's light.

The annunciation

So that this is not only words, I would like to see the annunciation reenacted in church with simple movements and a minimum of dramatic directions, so that as it is watched by the congregation it could be remembered and also reenacted in the home. Mary's last lines, "Behold, the handmaid of the Lord; let it be done to me according to your word," can then become the personal prayer of everyone who enacts it: a prayer for purification and an open, receptive attitude to the workings of God in his or her life. Let it be as an opening of the knots of our fear to indeed greet the Christ in whatever form he comes. When we act out a story, the meaning enters far more deeply into us than if we were simply hearing it in a passive way.

Here are some simple directions for the annunciation reading. Before the narration begins Mary would be seen seated, or kneeling, in a position of meditation or repose in front of the altar. It would be dramatically and spiritually effective at this point for a chorus of dancers to stand at some distance from her and pray in movement the "Let the clouds . . . " sequence described above. It would be the prayer of all people's longing for this unbelievable event. It would be additionally effective, if the prayer is included here, for everyone to have prayed it at the opening of the liturgy, so that it becomes a leitmotif, or recurring theme, in which all participate.

Then, as the narration begins, the angel Gabriel runs in, down the aisles, wheeling around until he comes to a stop, kneeling at just the right distance from Mary—not too close, not too far away, as in the old paintings where the distance between the eyes of Mary and Gabriel always seems just right for perfect communication. He bows on the words "Hail, O favored one, the Lord is with you!" Mary becomes troubled and turns away with hesitancy and fear. Gabriel responds gently, perhaps moving behind her and touching her shoulders as he says the lines (or as they are read by the narrator) "Do not be afraid, Mary . . . " He might lift her to her feet and lead her around as if showing her visions and new horizons as he continues, exclaiming, "He will be great . . . and of his kingdom there will be no end." Mary turns to the angel as she questions, "How can this be, since I have no husband?" And the angel blesses her with his hands while saying, "The Holy Spirit will come upon you . . . "

The final important gesture is on Mary's response: "Behold, I

am the handmaid of the Lord; let it be done to me according to
your word." The person who portrays Mary should work very
slowly and prayerfully to find this movement, experimenting with
different gestures until she feels one to be absolutely right for
her as a response. I suggest one slow movement that is a self-
offering—an offering of heart and soul and body to the Lord.

The following is a meditation dance to the Hail, Mary. It will need
some practice and careful attention paid to the description below,
so I offer it to those people in a congregation who have the time
and want to pray more deeply and fully with their bodies. It is
first of all movement for meditation and not primarily composed
of descriptive gestures, though there are some. The dance is simple enough for nonprofessional dancers to perform. It evolved
slowly with a friend, Martha, several years ago. It could be offered
in church, perhaps as a response to the annunciation sequence, or
done as a personal prayer in the home.

Opening position: Sitting on heels, back straight, palms resting
on knees, open.

Hail, Mary. Extend your right hand forward and up, ending at
your shoulder. (This is a circular motion, from out to in.) The
torso leans slightly back.

full of grace. The position of your right hand remains the same.
Draw your left hand up, close to your body, past your left shoulder and upward and out, as the torso leans backward. Continue
this circular motion until your left hand touches the floor in front
of you. Your torso bows forward, head close to the floor.

the Lord is with you. Rise onto your knees, extending your
arms overhead, face lifted.

Blessed are you among women. Sink back to your heels and
cross your arms in front of your chest, which is curved slightly
forward.

and blessed is the fruit of your womb, Jesus. As you sink onto
your heels, your hands uncross and your palms spread across your
navel ("womb"), moving sideways several inches from your center.
Return your hands to the center until your fingers touch, and in
a continuous movement arch your fingers outward, opening your
hands and extending your arms fully to the sides. Your torso is
lifted, head slightly back. Pause.

Holy Mary. Lean forward with a straight back, at about a forty-five degree angle, as your arms rise to a parallel line overhead, palms facing downward.

mother of God. Your torso leans backward as your arms descend and continue back of your body, circling up and over, ending with your torso in a complete forward bow. Palms face downward on the floor.

pray for us sinners. Hold the previous position.

now. Your palms turn upward. The rest of your body holds still.

and at the hour of our death. Return to the opening position, palms resting on knees, open and facing upward, torso straight.

Amen. With a small circular motion bring your hands to a prayer position, fingers pointing upward, palms together at chest level.

"O Come, O Come, Emmanuel"

Returning to suggestions for the whole congregation, one of my favorite dances for Advent, to be done as an entrance procession, is to "O Come, O Come, Emmanuel." It is a processional dance with wreath, to be done each week of Advent. All who want to try this will line up in pairs at the back of the church. One person is the leader and stands at the head of the double line. He or she will hold the advent wreath (which contains four unlit candles) at shoulder height, arms outstretched.

O Come, O Come, Emmanuel, and ransom captive Israel. On the words, "O Come, O Come . . . " the procession moves down the aisle, arms stretched in front, palms face upward. (Practice holding the arms out in such a way as to really feel them as an extension of the self seeking God.)

that mourns in lowly exile here. Leader with the wreath stops, and all the rest bow from the waist, lowering arms. (At this point in the third verse the sequence is changed. See later directions.)

until the son of God appear. All raise their bodies and lift up arms as before.

(Chorus) *Rejoice! Rejoice! Emmanuel.* The double line separates by everyone turning to face his partner and at the same time taking a big step backward, opening arms wide to the sides in a joyful manner. A pathway is thus formed down which the leader dances with the wreath. (It is easy to improvise with a wreath in one's hands. Show it off, turning from side to side in a spirit of delight.) The leader must be at the head of the line again in time for the next words.

shall come to thee, O Israel. The leader continues in front dancing, as the rest link right elbows with their partners, holding their free arms raised, and swing around one time in the center of the aisle. They end with their arms down by their sides, in original lines.

Repeat the entire sequence described so far, progressing toward the altar, while all in the pews sing the second verse and chorus. By the third verse the leader places the wreath on the altar and the double line separates to the left and right and encircles the altar (leaving out the bowing). By the time of the third chorus, all are standing still facing the altar.

(Chorus—third time) *Rejoice! Rejoice! Emmanuel.* On "Rejoice, rejoice," all take a step in toward the altar, hands held, arms lifting up. On "Emmanuel" all back away, lowering arms, dropping hands, and then lifting arms back out to the side.

shall come to thee, O Israel. All turn in place, arms lifted. Pause. The priest lights the first candle (on second week he lights the second candle, etc.) and says a prayer for Advent. He then joins the group and they all circle around the altar, hands joined, as the next verse is sung, or simply hummed. The chorus movements are repeated as before (stepping toward the altar, arms raised, etc.) and all then slowly file off to their places in the church, as a final verse and chorus is sung. The wreath is left on the altar, or placed in a special spot.

Repeat this processional dance each week, teaching more and more people the dance. I've led this with children and with adults. It takes about fifteen to twenty minutes to teach and is easier each week as more and more people join in. A comfortable number to start with is about six or eight people plus leader, and the number will probably double after a few times. All who dance should also join in the singing at least on the choruses. Singing out the word "Rejoice!" helps the movement to be strong.

Praying at home

To conclude, here are some suggestions for praying at home (in addition, many of those already described can be used at home).

Each week, as the candles of the advent wreath are lit and all are gathered, the members of the family in turn cup their hands over the flame and "draw" the warmth and light of the fire toward themselves—each to heart, face and then upward, in a wordless gesture of praise and offering.

Reflecting on the idea with which we began—Advent growing from a solo dance to a quartet—the first week, after the one candle is lit, all could stand in stillness, meditating on the light within and his or her hopes and fears. The second week, those present could take partners and pray together, strengthening their individual lights. The third week, groups of threes could form and, with hands joined, dance in circles, singing simple songs that reflect the increased light and energy flowing among them. The fourth week, four people, or all present, could join hands and pray to be truly a family that reflects the birth of Christ.

One last suggestion for family prayer: As a transition from Advent to Christmas and the present-giving rush, there could be a gift-wrapping prayer ceremony in which prayers are said for each person who will receive a gift, perhaps concluding with the song "It's a Gift to be Simple," and dancing with a spirit of lightheartedness.

CHRISTMAS

Christmas is a time when the ordinary routines of life are set aside, and people look for special, beautiful ways to celebrate the birth of Christ. It is, therefore, an ideal time to introduce gestures and dances in the liturgy, or as part of celebrations outside of the liturgy. People sing and dance when love overflows, and this is the season of love.

The visitation

Words and Music by Nick Hodsdon; dances created and described by Carla De Sola. Music follows on pages 49-55.

The second joyful mystery of the rosary is about Mary's visit with her cousin Elizabeth, as described in Luke 1:39-56. This is the only major New Testament passage dealing exclusively with women; the women are there doing their own thing, and are not just there as adjuncts to the activities of men. It's about a nice, a very human and a very simple event, a visit. Mary and Elizabeth are sharing together their wonder and joy at the anticipation they both feel on the coming birth of their first children—in both cases, an event which was certainly unexpected under these particular circumstances.

This "hora-torio" celebrates this event in *movement,* as Mary moved out on a major journey to see her cousin; in *musical conversation* between the two women, drawn directly from the scripture because half of the first chapter of Luke is drawn from old songs; and it ends with Mary's "Magnificat," the second part of which is to be danced as a *hora.* Mary was at the time a young Jewish girl who probably loved to dance *horas* in her home town of Nazareth. It could be done with dancers taking the parts of Mary and Elizabeth while singers sing their lines, or the dances could be modified and the singers could play the parts themselves. Accompaniment could be by guitar, or by piano or organ, or by guitar with xylophone or oboe or flute picking out embellishments written in the piano score.

A note on the "Magnificat": The religious songs (or psalms) of the ancient Hebrews often used the theme of God's bringing about justice through the "reversal of fortune"—the poor are exalted, the proud are made lowly. One psalm of national thanksgiving that was not included in the book of Psalms employs this theme, and in one of its reversal-of-fortune examples it says: "The barren woman has born sevenfold, but the mother of many is desolate." Around 500 B.C., an editor of the Hebrew scriptures inserted this psalm into the much older story of Hannah, the mother of the prophet Samuel (1 Samuel 2:1-10). Like Sarah, Rebeccah, Rachel, and later Elizabeth, Hannah had been barren until, in her later years, she conceived a child as a special sign of God's favor. In such cases, the unusual birth was taken as a symbol of the unusual importance of the child (viz., Isaac, Jacob, Joseph, and John the Baptist) in history.

In the New Testament, when Mary visits Elizabeth, Luke inserts a beautiful old canticle based on the song given to Hannah, beginning with the same theme of praise ("My soul magnifies the Lord . . . "), touching on the special favor of God in granting a very special first child (" . . . he has regarded the low estate of his handmaiden. . . . henceforth all generations will call me blessed . . . "), and again celebrating God's justice in reversal of fortune (" . . . he has put down the mighty . . . he has filled the hungry . . . ") This is one of four old songs with which Luke, the most poetic of the evangelists, has enriched the first chapter of his gospel.

Mary's song is called the "Magnificat" because this is the first word of the Latin translation: *"Magnificat anima mea Dominum."* The first part, to be sung in this setting by Mary alone, is a more personal song of praise than its prototypes (Hannah's song, or Psalm 113). The second part, to be sung here by a group of people as others dance the *hora,* is a triumphant celebration of God's goodness and faithfulness to "all generations who honor him."

Music is found on the pages following the spoken texts and movement descriptions. *—Nick Hodsdon*

Part I—Mary's Journey
"I will walk in the presence of the Lord"

NARRATOR: When the angel Gabriel came to Mary, she was troubled and confused to hear that she would bear a son, since she was a virgin. To reassure her and to give her a sign that nothing was impossible for God, the angel told her that her cousin Elizabeth, although she was in her old age and was thought to be barren, was also going to bear a child and was already in her sixth month! So Mary set out to visit her cousin.

The movements: As the words to Part I ("*I will walk in the presence . . .* ") are sung, Mary is slowly walking through the church ultimately heading toward Elizabeth who is in the pulpit or behind the altar, unseen. She walks with her head and chest lifted, as if in anticipation of their joyful meeting. She is seen to call Elizabeth and to listen delightedly to the echoes bouncing off the mountains.

After she stops and calls a third time, Mary stands motionless as Elizabeth bursts into view. We see her calling, "Mary!" Her arms are stretched out in a big welcome gesture.

Performance notes: (1) A voice in the back of the church may sing Mary's part with a voice in the front singing Elizabeth, or the dance could be simplified and the dancers portraying Mary and Elizabeth could sing themselves.

(2) The "Echo" voices, one on the left and one on the right,

could turn their backs, or place cupped hands in front of mouths.

(3) Mary walks on "I will . . . living," stops when calling Elizabeth and listens to the echoes. The third time Elizabeth appears and answers her.

Part II—Elizabeth's Greeting
"Blest are you among all women"

NARRATOR: And when Elizabeth heard the greeting of Mary, the babe leaped in her womb and Elizabeth was filled with the Holy Spirit.

The movements: During the narration, Elizabeth draws her arms toward her womb with a backward impulse starting from her stomach, as if feeling the movement of the child. The impulse starts her turning in place, lifting her arms and head higher and higher in exultation. Mary then runs to Elizabeth, who is in front of the altar, and embraces her.

NARRATOR: And Elizabeth said, . . .

The movements: On the words *"Blessed are you among all women,"* Mary sinks down, sitting on her heels, facing away from the congregation, with her arms wrapped around Elizabeth's knees, while Elizabeth, in a gesture of extended blessing in slow motion, brings her arms down to her sides, backward, overhead and forward over Mary.

On *"Why this honor God has granted me? The mother of my Lord should come to me?"* Elizabeth raises her head and one arm upward as if to God, and then draws Mary up to her feet. Now Elizabeth responds more playfully. On the words, *"The moment I heard you,"* Elizabeth takes two large steps backward, raising her arms. On *"the babe in my womb,"* she steps together, bending her knees, touches her womb, and, coming to her toes, brings her hands up as if showing the child leaping toward Mary.

On *"he leaped up in joy and I danced 'round the room,"* with her arms overhead, Elizabeth takes four skipping steps to the other side of Mary.

On *"how blest is the woman believing in God,"* they take each other's hands and, swinging away from the congregation, each turns in place, letting go of their hands when they are back to back, and taking hands again when they face each other.

On *"he keeps every promise, no matter how odd,"* they lean back, and, holding hands, they spin around.

On *"Oh, Mary!"* Elizabeth embraces Mary, knowing that Mary is experiencing the same anticipation of bearing her first child.

Part III—Mary's Song of Praise
The Magnificat

As the music begins, Mary is on the left hand side of Elizabeth, and slightly downstage. Mary and Elizabeth move a little apart and take hands upstage.

On *"My heart rejoices in my savior,"* Mary makes an arc with her left hand, first up toward her heart, curving her chest inward, then extending her hand toward Elizabeth, and then away from her and upward, while turning toward the congregation, with palms up, as if offering her heart to God. She is lifted high on her toes at this point.

On *"my soul proclaims my Lord on high,"* she lowers her left hand and brings both arms up overhead, palms facing toward her, and takes several steps forward at the same time, ending on her toes. She lowers to her heels, passing her arms in front of her face while lifting her face with a sense of reverence. In a continuous motion she lowers to one knee and extends her arms out to the sides with palms forward, raising her head even higher. On *"he saw this simple lowly serving maid,"* she brings the other knee down, and, sinking back on her heels, lowers her body forward, arms on the floor in front of her head, palms facing upward.

On *"now, always, everyone shall know my joy,"* Mary rises to her knees, makes a half turn to the left, pivoting on her right knee, ending with her left leg forward, and continuing the turn she comes to standing, facing the congregation again, lifting her chest slowly all the while, and walks forward toward the congregation. On the word *"joy,"* she turns upstage to face Elizabeth, and both raise their hands overhead at the same time, smiling at each other.

On *"for he who is mighty has lifted me high,"* Mary skips four times upstage, left of Elizabeth.

On *"the holiest name any angel could cry!"* she continues

skipping, turning to the left in a small circle around herself. She claps her hands on the first and third skips, raising them on the second and fourth skips.

On *"to all those who fear him, who honor that name,"* she continues skipping, returning to downstage center, all the while raising her hands slowly in front of her, palms facing out.

On *"his mercy unfolds, generations the same,"* she takes four steps turning to the left in place, and slowly lowers her arms to her sides. Mary is beginning to see the vision of the generations praising God.

On *"all people,"* she extends her right arm to the right side of the congregation, and the dancers sitting there rise from their pews.

On *"forever,"* she extends her left hand to the left side of the congregation, and the dancers sitting there rise in the same way. They come forward and up to the altar area on the connecting music, forming two lines toward the back on each side of the altar. Mary lowers her arms and walks forward.

Part IV—Mary's Vision
A joyful hora

On *"he has shown the power of his arm . . . "* the two lines from opposite sides of the altar walk past each other to form a circle around Mary by the end of the words " *. . . kings from their thrones."* While doing this they hold hands, each line following a leader, and walk with a "step-bend, step-bend" movement: (step right, bend right knee; step left, bend left knee; etc.). They end by forming one circle around Mary and, holding hands, raise their arms high.

On the repeat of *"he has shown the power of his arm . . . "* all do the *hora* step—step side to the left with the left foot and cross the right foot in back of the left foot. Jump together, landing on both feet, and kick the right foot in front, pointing it a little to the left. Jump together and now kick the left foot in front, pointing it to the right. Repeat this sequence over and over again.

On the repeat of *"he has swept away the kings from their thrones,"* all finish the last *hora* step, step left and then *turn* in place to the left. (This "paddle turn" is done by stepping on the left foot in place, and turning by pushing around with the right foot.)

On *"he has filled the hungry with his goodness,"* every other person in the circle comes toward Mary with four steps, moving as before with knees bending and straightening. They hold their arms extended in front, palms up, as if honoring Mary's "fullness." Mary extends her arms to them in a "welcome" and "giving" gesture.

On the lines *"he has lifted up the humble and the low,"* they step backward to their previous places in the circle while the others come forward in the same way. Mary welcomes them, too, turning slowly in place while doing so.

On *"he has come to help his servant, Israel,"* they back away and join the rest. All form little groups of twos or threes, with arms on each other's shoulders, or stretched upward in different positions of praise and closeness to one another.

As this is happening, Mary, in the center, crosses her arms in front of her chest with a swing motion, drops them and raises her arms up high overhead, and drops to one knee, bowing and lowering her arms.

On *"remembering his promise to our father, Abraham,"* Mary slowly rises, head up, arms lifting high, as all the rest circle in place with their partners or group, sustaining the different gestures.

On *"he's remembering, his mercies numbering, his saving love to all his sons forevermore,"* all, including Mary, do the *hora* steps.

On the coda (*"he has shown the power of his arm . . . "*), all file off following one leader down the center aisle, repeating the beginning "step-bend" movement. Mary raises her hand high to wave to them and comes to stillness as the "vision of all generations" recedes. She then slowly lowers her hand and turns it into a gesture toward Elizabeth, and they come together as the narrator speaks.

NARRATOR: Mary stayed with Elizabeth about three months, and then returned to her own home.

The choir repeats the first phrases of Part I (*"I will walk in the presence of the Lord, in the land of the living"*), and Mary and Elizabeth slowly walk off, arm in arm, smiling into each other's eyes.

HORA-TORIO The Second Joyful Mystery
("I will walk in the presence of the Lord")

Part 1:
Mary's Journey

words and music
by Nick Hodsdon

49

As narrator reads *Luke* 1:41, Elizabeth dances.

Part 2:
Elizabeth's Greeting ("Blest are you among women . . .")

grant - ed me; the moth - er of my Lord should come to me! The mo-ment I heard you, the babe in my womb, he leaped up in joy and I danced 'round the room! How blest is the wom-an be - liev - ing in God! He keeps eve-ry prom - ise, no mat - ter how odd! Oh Mar - y

Playfully (with a twinkle in her eye)

rall.

Ritenuto, lento, tenderly

Ritenuto, lento, tenderly

51

52

Part 4:
Mary's Vision of "All Generations" (A Joyful Hora)

Music and lyrics © by Nick Hodsdon, 1974.

Happypageant

I would like to see the day when every church has a resident musician and dancer creating for the services to everyone's heart's delight. It's so delightful for a dancer to have a live musician to work with, and I imagine that a musician would find it delightful too. "Singers and dancers alike say, 'All my springs are in you'" (Psalm 87). Nick Hodsdon, a young guitarist-singer who plays and composes for a variety of Catholic and Protestant churches in New York (and likes to dance, too) wrote some music and came up with a scriptural narration and a dramatic scheme for a nativity pageant.

The "Happypageant," first appearing in *Liturgy* in 1972, has been performed with great success on several occasions that we know of, including a midnight service in a Methodist church in Brooklyn, and an Episcopal children's service in New York City. Both groups felt free to make adaptations to fit their particular needs. Anybody, young and old together, could learn and present the easy folk-style songs and dances described here as a Christmas offering, or as a service of "Lessons and Carols."

(Lights come up on Mary and Joseph in the stable, at front of the sanctuary.)

NARRATOR: (Luke 2:1-7)

While Mary and Joseph do a lullaby-rocking dance, they (or another man and woman or men and women) sing Song 1, "Lullaby" from an old German folksong).

Song 1

Mary: Joseph dear, O Joseph mine, help me rock the
Joseph: Glad - ly will I, Ma - ry mine, help you rock the

babe di - vine, And on us God's light/love will shine; so
babe di - vine, And on us God's light/love will shine; so

slum - ber now, lul - lay, the son of Ma - ry. _____
slum - ber now, lul - lay, the son of Ma - ry. _____

Dance 1: "Lullaby"—Mary kneels in front, sitting on her heels and facing the congregation, with arms curved in front of her. She is absorbed in rocking her baby. Joseph is standing in back. Mary looks back toward him; he walks forward, kneels, puts his arms gently around her and helps rock the child. On *"and on us God's light will shine . . . "* Mary slowly lifts up her arms and face, with a feeling of awe and praise. She then bends forward over Joseph and the baby with a gesture of peace and protection. On the second verse, both Mary and Joseph rock the baby together. On *"and on us . . . "* both come to their knees, raising hands as if lifting the baby up to God and for the whole world to see. They then slowly return to their cradling position, looking at one another with love.

(Always start directing these dances by asking the dancer to show how he would rock a baby; walk like a camel; be a shining star. Do what feels natural!)

(Lights come up on the shepherds, at some other part of the church.)

NARRATOR: (Luke 2:8-10a)

ANGEL: "Be not afraid; for behold, I bring you good news of a great joy which will come to all the people; for to you is born this day in the city of David a Savior, who is Christ the Lord. And this will be a sign for you: you will find a babe wrapped in swaddling cloths and lying in a manger" (Luke 2:10b-12).

NARRATOR continues after music has been established for Song 2, "Alleluia chant" (adapted by Nick Hodsdon from the Hare Krishna Chant).

Song 2

Narrator: (spoken)   And suddenly

(all sing, while Shepherds dance)
there was with the angel a multitude of the heavenly host praising God and saying, Glo - ry,

glo - ry, ___ glo - ry, glo - ry, ___ to ___ God ___ in the

high __ est. ___ Peace on earth, ___ Peace on earth, ___ good __

will ___ to ___ men. ___ Al - le - lu - ia, ___ Al - le

lu - ia, ___ Al - le - lu - ia, ___ al - le - lu - ia! ___ - al - le

©1972 Nick Hodsdon

(Repeat "Alleluia" measures ad lib, then segue into Song 3, "Wyo.")

Dance 2: Shepherds' dance to "Alleluia Chant"—When the lights come up, before the narrator starts, the shepherds are playing on imaginary flutes, calling to their sheep, gazing at the stars, etc. One could yawn and stretch. As the angel of the Lord approaches, the shepherds huddle together with heads turned toward the angel in fear and then in amazement as he speaks to them. As the word *"Glory"* is first sung, one shepherd (the leader) rises and begins to whirl with joy, turning in place with arms open, gradually lifting them up high. On *"Peace on earth . . ."* he raises the other shepherds up, one after the other, and they begin to whirl. All join hands on *"Alleluia,"* to form a circle, and, leaning way back, move clockwise with the grapevine step (step side to the left with the left foot, cross the right foot in front and stop; step side to the left again and cross the right foot in back, and so on.) Keep chest and face lifted. On the fifth *"alleluia,"* all come to the center of the circle with both arms raised, palms facing center, with a feeling of praise, and then back away to original circle. Do this in-and-out movement twice.

(Accompanist establishes 4/4 time in key of C major.)

(Shepherds get themselves together, ad libbing something like "Let's all go to Bethlehem and see what's happened!" etc. [Luke 2:15]. Then all sing Song 3, "Wyo," while dancing to the stable scene to join Mary and Joseph.)

Song 3

©1972 Nick Hodsdon

4. Kings are comin'! Glory be! Wy-o, let's go an' see!
   They comin', one and two and three, they comin' to the manger! *(Chorus)*

5. Angel singin', "Come with me!" Wy-o, let's go an' see!
   He say, "This baby hold the key, who's lyin' in the manger!" *(Chorus)*

6. "He come, he show how men be free." Wy-o, let's go an' see!
   "He come, he show what life should be; he's lyin' in the manger." *(Chorus)*

Dance 3: "Wyo, Let's Go and See"—The leader of the shepherds begins by moving away from the others with a step-kick movement to the music. On the first *"Wyo,"* he turns back to the others and gestures for them to join him. They all form a chain, doing the same step-kick movement, behind him. On the chorus, all form a star, as in square dancing, by joining right hands together. (Form two stars if there are more than four or five shepherds.) Dancing in a circle this way, they lean out, with left arms raised high, palms

59

facing forward, as if following a star. All quickly reverse directions for the second half of the chorus (left hands in center, right arms raised). Repeat this same pattern of a chain and then star formation for verses two and three, all the while progressing happily toward the stable. They end by sitting quietly around Mary and Joseph.

(The last time, the chorus is sung softly, as lights go down on the manger scene and come up on the three kings with their camels and their star, at some other part of the church. They process slowly toward manger scene, singing Song 4, "I've been a-wand-'ring" [by Nick Hodsdon, using a theme from Feste's Song in Twelfth Night].)

(Accompanist establishes slow 6/8 time in the key of A minor while Narrator reads.)

NARRATOR: Now when Jesus was born in Bethlehem of Judea in the days of Herod the king, behold, wise men from the East came to Jerusalem, saying:

KING: "Where is he who has been born king of the Jews? For we have seen his star in the East, and have come to worship him" (Matthew 2:1-2).

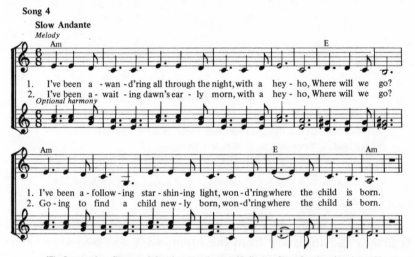

Song 4

Slow Andante

1. I've been a - wan - d'ring all through the night, with a hey - ho, Where will we go?
2. I've been a - wait - ing dawn's ear - ly morn, with a hey - ho, Where will we go?

1. I've been a - follow - ing star - shin - ing light, won - d'ring where the child is born.
2. Go - ing to find a child new - ly born, won - d'ring where the child is born.

(The Star may have finger cymbals; others may ring camel bells, etc. Sing a few times in unison; add parts only if it gets monotonous. Add highest part if you have a tremendous distance to cover.)

©1972 Nick Hodsdon

Dance 4: "I've Been A-Wand'ring"—All during this song, the dancer who is the star of Bethlehem leads the three kings, each with a camel in front of him, slowly toward the stable. (You might use the center aisle for this procession.) The kings walk slowly and stately, holding reins with the left hand and looking upward toward a star. Right hand is raised toward it. The three dancers who are the camels move bent slightly over, rocking and swaying in front of their king. The Star, who is in front, holds little bells or finger cymbals high overhead. He rings them as he moves smoothly forward on tiptoe, turning every now and then. The kings keep processing to about ten feet from the manger scene, then stop.

NARRATOR: . . . they went their way: and lo, the star which they had seen in the East went before them, till it came to rest over the place where the child was. (*Star leaves kings and moves behind Mary and Joseph.*) When they saw the star, they rejoiced exceedingly with great joy! (Matthew 2:9-10).

(Kings hear a bell, then another, then a whole bunch of them, ringing louder and louder from the manger scene. The shepherds, etc., begin to chant the word "alleluia," each at his own tempo, quietly at first and then more and more joyfully. Finally all break into the fourth verse of Song 3, "Wy-o.")

Dance 4, Part Two: Kings dance to "Wyo, let's go and see"— *During verse four,* the kings and camels come forward, and they lay their gifts (if you decide to include this part of the tradition) before the manger. On the chorus and through verse five, the kings are so happy they cavort around; each king has a funny step or trick (somersaults, cartwheels, clicking heels together, etc.)— whatever the dancer likes to do best. Enough of these eternally somber "wise men"! *During verse six,* various barnyard animals may dance out and around to "see this thing that has come to pass." Direct each child (or adult!) who wants to be an animal to choose one characteristic of the animal with which to portray it. (For example, the child dancing a pigeon might make a pecking motion with hand or head; a rabbit might hop and wiggle his ears, bringing fourteen carrots, gold. The cat could myrrh contentedly. The sleepy donkey could be frankly incensed at the disturbance.)

(After last chorus, all segue into the "Alleluia" measures of Song 2, "Alleluia Chant.")

Dance 5: All dance to the "Alleluia Chant"—During the chant the kings and shepherds and animals form two concentric circles around Mary and Joseph and the Star. One circle moves clockwise and the other counterclockwise. All walk joyfully, holding hands and leaning backward, arms upraised. On the last "alleluia" they turn in place, each in his own style.

(The chant gets fuller and fuller; congregation may join in; then gradually fades away as animals, shepherds and kings bid farewell and leave Mary and Joseph to sing the child to sleep. The Star remains, shining over them.)

NARRATOR: (Luke 2:20, 17-19)

(Mary and Joseph repeat the second verse movements of the rocking-lullaby dance while somebody sings both verses of Song 1, "Lullaby." As lights go out, we hear the bell of the Star of Bethlehem chiming softly.)

Christmas carols

Dancing at Christmastime, especially to carols, is quite traditional. I have read that the early meaning of "carol" was to move in a circle while singing. Doug Adams writes that "to carol" means "to dance," and that the term "stanza" means to stand, and "chorus" to dance. He suggests that everyone dance the chorus (this would be particularly easy when the melody and words are so familiar as in Christmas carols) and rest during the stanzas, or verses, which could be danced by a solo dancer, or trained group.

(See Doug Adams, *Involving the People in Dancing Worship, Historic and Contemporary Patterns,* Sacred Dance Guild, 1975.)

The "Cornwall Carol" which comes from the time of medieval minstrels and troubadours is sung by some folk singers today, and I have used it on occasion as a change from the more well-known "Lord of the Dance." It is included in Margaret Fisk Taylor's *A Time to Dance, Symbolic Movement in Worship* (Boston: United Church Press, 1967). It relates the life of Christ, from birth to resurrection, in a ballad form. The refrain is:

> Tomorrow shall be my dancing day,
> I would my true love did so chance
> To see the legend of my play,
> To call my true love to my dance.
>   Sing, O my love, O my love, my love, my love;
>   This have I done for my true love.

In the same book, Margaret Fisk Taylor notes that dancing was part of the medieval Christmas carol "Joseph Dearest, Joseph Mine" (which is included, coincidentally, in the "Happypageant" described above). There were apparently symbolic movements of rocking the Christ child in the cradle. She adds that another custom involved putting a doll (representing again the Christ child) on the altar on Christmas eve. Children would then dance a ring dance around it.

Several years ago the Omega Dance Group in New York City began the custom of singing and dancing Christmas carols on the streets a few days before Christmas eve. Gathering at a corner, we would sing and dance and invite passersby to join us. Then we would move on to another location, usually skipping there while singing "Jingle Bells," and start over again. (We had great fun, even when it rained one year, and found that people enjoyed the momentary break from their last-minute Christmas shopping rush). Having a good song leader along was essential so that the dancers were free to put full energy into their movements and could encourage new people to join in without the music stopping.

Below are movement suggestions set to six well-known carols. Two of the examples are particularly suitable for liturgical occasions; the rest are good for street carolling or family or school celebrations.

O Come, All Ye Faithful

"O Come, All Ye Faithful" lends itself to a processional style dance, with devotional movements for everyone on the chorus. The chorus ("O come, let us adore him") with its movements could be used separately as a special liturgical gesture or response of adoration during the whole Christmas season.

As the verse begins (*"O come, all ye faithful, joyful and triumphant," etc.*) the presider, along with others carrying banners, candles, incense, crucifix, and so on, slowly move down the aisle. On the first line of the chorus (*"O come, let us adore him"*) all stand in place and the presider bows, either still facing the direction the procession is moving in, or turning and bowing facing the people. On the second "O come, let us adore him" all the rest of the procession bow and the presider repeats his gesture. On the third repeat, the priest and people in the procession and congregation bow together.

An alternative way would be for the presider to bow once, facing the congregation, and hold his position (torso bent forward), for *half* the congregation to bow on the second "O come, let us adore him" and hold their position, and then the other half of the congregation to bow on the final "O come, let us adore him." (This would not have to include a procession beforehand.) The effect would be like waves of adoration. All would rise together in response to the words *"Christ the Lord!"*

All the bows could be done simply, just bending forward from the waist, arms gesturing forward and lowering to the sides, or with a slight lift. This is done by first rising to the balls of the feet and gesturing upward with the arms, then lowering the arms and curving the torso forward and over and bending the knees as you sink to your heels. This imparts a feeling of breath and spirit to the movement. When the priest gestures on his bow he can best express the intention of inviting all to join him by emphasizing the forward movement of his arms.

Silent Night

"Silent Night" could be done in church, perhaps during the liturgy as a special way to usher in the kiss of peace, or as part of the Christmas carolling in the streets or in the home.

The formation is a circle, facing counterclockwise, of about six to eight people. All hold candles in their right hands and place their left hands on the left shoulder of the person in front of them.

On *"Silent Night,"* all step forward with the right foot, and then with the left foot. Repeat on *"holy night."* On *"all is calm"* step forward with the right foot with a small lunge (the right knee is bent) and hold through "calm." On *"all is bright"* step or shift back to the left foot, leaning backward (bending the left knee) and hold. The face is uplifted, as if seeing the lovely night.

Repeat this entire pattern of four steps and two lunges during the next line (*"round yon virgin, mother and child, holy infant so tender and mild"*).

On *"sleep in heavenly peace"* all face the center of the circle and lower their candles to the middle. The candles lift upward as the last note of "peace" rises. On the final "sleep in heavenly peace" all turn to the right and face the outside of the circle, each holding the candle with both hands, lowered to about shoulder height. (This would be the peace gesture to precede the kiss of peace if done during the liturgy.)

Note: I have also had children take the roles of Mary, Joseph, the star, shepherds, angels and animals and create a simple pageant-like dance to it, similar to the "Happypageant." Mary and Joseph start in the center rocking the baby (a live child), the star is twinkling behind them, and the angels call to the shepherds in the fields (running joyously to them), who become the wise men and bow and present gifts to the child. What needs to be set up beforehand (like ground rules) is the place that each child begins from. For example, if the angels start in one corner, the shepherds would begin in another. It is also important to outline the path they are to follow in order to reach the manger.

Deck the Halls

This is suitable for street carolling or as a pre-Christmas tree decorating dance.

The formation is two concentric circles. One circle faces clockwise and the other counterclockwise. All participants hold wreaths or other Christmas ornaments in their hands.

On the first line (*"Deck the halls with boughs of holly"*) through the *"fa la la's"* all skip eight times (or walk forward with a bouncy step). The circles are moving in opposite directions. The wreaths are held high, overhead. On the second line ("*'t'is the season to be jolly," etc.*) everyone sharply turns around and skips in the opposite direction. On *"don we now our gay apparel"* all face center and skip four times forward, and on the *"fa la la la la's"* all skip backward four times. On *"troll the ancient yule-tide carol"* all turn in place to the right, and on the final *"fa la la's"* all face center and sway (shift weight) first to the right and then to the left. Begin again, inviting more people to join in.

Hark! The Herald Angels Sing

This is also for street carolling. The formation is two straight lines, as in the "Virginia Reel," partners facing one another.

On *"Hark! the herald angels sing"* all move toward their partners with four steps. Hands are held as if blowing a trumpet (right hand to mouth, left hand farther away, fingers curled and facing in opposite directions). The chest is lifted, "trumpet" pointing upward. On *"glory to the new-born king"* all take four steps backward to original places. The torso lowers and the "trumpet" points downward. On *"peace on earth, and mercy mild, God and sinners reconciled"* the same pattern is repeated, but done with a "do-si-do" step. (In the "do-si-do" you pass your partner by the right shoulder, step sideways to the right and then step backward, passing your partner's left shoulder.)

On *"joyful all you nations rise . . . "* up to the final *"Hark! the herald angels sing"* partners join hands and slide down the center in the following way: the first person in each line comes to the center, takes his partner's both hands and chassés, or slides, down the center. They peel off when they reach the end of the line, one person turning to the right and the other to the left and walk back to place. Everyone chassés down the line in the same fashion until the original couple is once again at the head. On the final refrain (*"Hark! the herald angels sing, glory to the new-born king"*), all link right elbows with their partners and circle in a clockwise direction, then change direction and circle in the opposite direction, left elbows linked. Repeat the dance adding clapping and flourishes.

Jingle Bells

This is done while skipping down the street to a new location. On the verses (*"Dashing through the snow,"* *etc.*) all move down the street, skipping, running, weaving in and out of one another, kicking heels up behind and moving arms up and down or in a pinwheel fashion. Bells should be ringing.

On the chorus all stand still and ring bells from head to toe by slowly lowering and raising the torso. All jump on *"hey!"* This repeats twice as follows:

Jingle bells! Jingle bells! Jingle all the way! (torso lowers while hands are ringing the bells).

Oh, what fun it is to ride in a one-horse open sleigh! Hey! (torso and arms rise, with bells still ringing, then, jump).

Finish the second chorus with arms around one another's shoulders. Either start a new dance or continue with the verse, skipping with arms held in this position, three or four abreast.

This description seems to be the reverse of the old "chorus" (move), "stanza" (stand still) suggestion described above. The dance could also be done by skipping to a new location on the chorus and standing still, singing, on the verses.

You Take Our Hands

Danced to the music of "Greensleeves," this is for street carolling and parties; a slightly more advanced technique is required.

"Greensleeves" is such an engaging melody that it appears with various texts. Most people know the lovely Christmas carol "What Child is This?" This could be sung softly, all standing in place, and then the following dance take place, to the music of "Greensleeves," but with original words by Kathleen Jenks:

> You take our hands,
> You call us friends
> and dance with us through the streets of the world.
> "Go out," you say, "find my sheep and tend
> them til I come again—
>   Dance, dance, my peace be with you,
>   sing and praise in the streets of the world.
>   Trust my love through the shadows of earth
>   and dance open your hearts for my birth.

The formation is a circle, with partners standing side by side.

Everyone faces to the right, or counterclockwise, holding inside hands low, outside hand above shoulder height, palms touching.

On *"You take our hands"* partners open outward (still holding inside hands) and balancé apart (like a waltz step, but a down, up, down) starting with the outside foot. The outside arms fan open. On *"you call us friends"* partners come back together with the same step (starting on the inside leg) and touch the palms of the outside hand together (fingertips pointing upward). This pattern is repeated on the third line (*"and dance with us through the streets of the world"*). Balancé four times in all.

On *"'Go out,' you say, 'find my sheep and tend'"* couples face one another, with both hands joined. They step to the right (inside person to the left, so that both move together in the same counterclockwise direction), bring the left (or right) foot to the right (or left) foot, then chassé one time in the same direction and step out again to the right (or inside person's left) and pause. The entire pattern is repeated in the opposite direction (clockwise). While doing these steps and chassés, or slides, arms move in a swaying manner, hands clasped with partner's. The hands can make a loop while sliding, ending stretched to the right (for the outside person; left for the inside person). The arm direction reverses with the pattern.

The final phrase (*"Dance, dance,"* etc.) is done in a strong, folk-like way, covering lots of space. The couples grasp both hands, as in ice-skating, and face counterclockwise. The step is as follows: All slide forward on the right foot and bring the left foot to meet it, then step forward again on the right foot and hop on it while at the same time kicking the left lower leg forward. This pattern repeats to the left. It is done six times in all. On *"and dance open your hearts for my birth"* the outside person (usually the woman) raises both arms overhead and turns, moving forward around the circle. She advances one person ahead on the inside circle, and he becomes her next partner. The inside people stand still during this phrase, or can turn in place. All begin again with new partners.

Pastores a Belen

This is a lovely, charmingly simple Christmas offertory dance that Sister Veronica Mendez created for the teenagers of St. Brigid's parish in New York City. I asked her to describe it.

Pastores a Belen vamos con alegria
Porque ha nacido ya el Hijo de Maria.
Alli, alli, nos espera Jesus;
Alli, alli, nos espera Jesus.
Llevemos pues turones y miel
Par' ofrecer al nino Manual.
Vamos, vamos, vamos a ver,
Vamos a ver al recien nacido,
Vamos a ver al nino Manuel.

Shepherds let us go to Bethlehem with joy
Because the Son of Mary is born.
There, there, Jesus waits for us;
There, there, Jesus waits for us.
Let us bring then nuggets and honey
To offer to the child Emmanuel.
Let us go, let us go, let us go see,
Let us go see the newly born,
Let us go see the child Emmanuel.

Pastores a Belen vamos con alegria. The shepherds walk eagerly,
with hands extended, in a wide zigzag as if they were winding
their way down the hills of Bethlehem, searching for the star and
the message it brings.

Porque ha nacido ya el Hijo de Maria. Arms are brought in as
if cradling a baby.

Alli, alli. Arms are moved in wide circular motions in front of
the face and body, as if trying to see the star more clearly.

nos espera Jesus. Arms are extended in front of the body,
expressing the eagerness with which Jesus waits for us.

Llevemos pues turones y miel / Par' ofrecer al nino Manuel.
(Repeat). One shepherd bends down to pick up nuggets and honey,
also wine and bread for the procession with the gifts; as he rises
he passes the items to the other shepherds until all have something
to carry.

*Vamos, vamos, vamos a ver, / Vamos a ver al recien nacido, /
Vamos a ver al nino Manuel.* A stately procession to the altar follows, everyone carrying gifts and moving to the beat of the "Vamos,
vamos." The shepherds carrying the wine and bread place them
on the altar; the ones carrying the nuggets and honey bow all the

way to the ground before the crib with their gifts extended and
then place them before the crib.

Pas - to - res a Be - len va - mos con a - le - gri - a Que

ha na - ci - do ya el Hi - jo de Ma - ri - a. — A - lli, a -

lli, nos es - pe - ra Je - sus; Lle - ve - mos pues tu - ro - nes y miel par'

o - fre - cer al ni - no Ma - nuel. Va - mos, va - mos, va - mos a ver,

va - mos a ver al re - cien na - ci - do, va - mos a ver al ni - no Ma - nuel.

LENT

Dance, in combination with prayer and scripture, enables people
to participate more directly in the transforming power of God.
And Lent is a time for transformation—for individuals, families,
communities.

Dance is a means of breaking down the isolation in life. It
relates people to their environment, including other people. It
serves to overcome restrictions in personal life, by encouraging
freedom to be self-expressive without guilt. It is a yoga in that
it assists to renew our relationship to life through movement and
gesture. It makes us both more conscious of ourselves and unself-
conscious at the same time. As self-consciousness diminishes, the
individual is able to transcend the limiting personal self and form
a creative link to that which is all, God.

In combination with prayer and scripture we have a context
for dance that greatly assists this development. Dancing to scripture makes us focus on eternal realities, yet the interpretation is
ever personal. We have the opportunity of linking the mysteries

of our inner life to the light of the word of God.

Our lenten self is like the dark earth hidden under the winter snow. Let us dig deep, draw close, not reflecting on the nature of ourselves or the beauties of scripture from a distance, but entering into our prayer "with every one of our limbs."

Following are dance-prayer suggestions for liturgical use (suitable for the entire congregation or for small groups), for lenten workshops, for a children's liturgy, and finally, suggestions for prayer in the home.

Here are two ways of praying the Lord, have mercy with our bodies. The first suggestion is for the whole congregation, the second for a small group that would have time to practice and perfect it, to create the same flow and calmness in the dance movements that is felt in the Gregorian chant.

Lord, have mercy

1. All are standing, with torsos bent over, arms held in any position of contrition (perhaps crossed over the chest). The people hold this position while the priest utters the first prayer of contrition. All respond by saying *Lord, have mercy* while holding their body position. This position is maintained during the second prayer of the priest, but all unfold their bodies ever so slightly while reciting the *Christ, have mercy*. They hold this new position during the third prayer of the priest, and on the final *Lord, have mercy* all completely unfold, opening their chests and arms into a position of receiving mercy.

In short, the movement-prayer is only an unfolding of the torso, reflecting in our bodies our feeling of contrition yet trust in the Lord's mercy. It is very simple yet helps all focus and be present to the Lord to whom we are speaking.

2. The following dance is set to the chant reproduced below. Each part is sung twice, first by the presider or cantor, then by all. The dance begins halfway down the aisle and moves slowly toward the altar. All follow the same direction.

Ky - ri - e   e   -   le - i - son.

Chri - ste   e   -   le - i - son.

As the first Kyrie is chanted, those participating will walk slowly down the aisle. Arms are held in front of the body at chest height, with palms facing up. As you walk, feel that your hands are asking for mercy, and actually receiving mercy. Be conscious of the space around you. Let its sacredness touch you.

As the Kyrie is repeated, lower your arms, bow deeply, place your hands on the floor, and, extending one leg after the other, lie on the floor, face down, hands supporting you under the shoulders.

As the Christe is chanted, beginning with your head, gradually raise your back (your hips remain on the floor). Pause.

Now, leaving your back raised, curl your lower legs to the right, and with your knees still on the floor, open them and make a half turn to the left, ending facing away from the altar. You are now sitting on the floor. Your right leg is in front of you and your left leg behind, knees bent.

While doing this turning movement, extend your arms out, palms facing up, as if pleading for the whole congregation. Then round your back over and opening your arms, bring them to the floor on either side of you, palms face down.

On the repeat of the Christe rise to your knees and bring your knees together) and then make a half turn to the left (facing the altar) by pivoting on the right knee. End with the left leg forward, knee up, foot on the floor in front of you. Stretch your arms out to the sides, at shoulder height, with palms facing forward. Hold this position, praying.

(This can be done in a simpler manner by omitting the turn. Rise to your knees and bring your left leg forward, knee high, and stretch arms to the sides as described.)

As the Kyrie chant begins again, slowly stand and walk forward as before, arms held at chest height in front of your body, palms face up. Walk slowly. *On the final Kyrie* slowly lower to your right knee in a bow, body bending forward, arms down by your sides. Pause in this position until the last note has passed.

Each church building presents a challenge as to how to use its space most effectively. If there is a long aisle, it is probably best to start the dance by moving up it, as I suggested here. If the altar is in the center of a round area, try having people start from all the different sides and converge toward the center. Experiment with lighting effects as well. Ask all who are not dancing to sing the repeat of each line after the presider.

The psalmist says "deep calls to deep." May this movement-meditation dance be as a voice from our depth calling to God for mercy.

Lines like these from Isaiah always stand out for me during Lent:

Lamb of God

> Is not this the fast that I choose:
>   to loose the bonds of wickedness,
>   to undo the thongs of the yoke,
> to let the oppressed go free, . . .
> Is it not to share your bread with the hungry,
>   and bring the homeless poor into your house . . .
>
>   —*Isaiah 58:6-7*

It occurred to me that these, the hungry and naked and poor, are the lambs of God, like the Lamb of God, loved by God who "will feed his flock like a shepherd, he will gather the lambs in his arms, he will carry them in his bosom . . . " (Isaiah 40).

Here is a simple way to dance our prayer to the Lamb of God, and an extension as suggested by Isaiah 58.

Lamb of God. Begin in a sitting position with your back straight, hands holding onto your shoulders. As the words start, slowly round your back over, using your hands to weigh you down. Actually pull your shoulders and back over with your hands.

You take away the sins of the world. Drop your hands (releasing the pressure on your back) and lower them in front of you, palms facing upward. As your hands drop, allow your back to respond by slowly straightening. (Practice this movement until you feel the coordination of being weighted with your hands and bent over, and then released and free—free, as it were, from the heaviness of sin.)

Have mercy on us. Reach (with your arms in front of your body) forward and upward, palms facing up. Since the prayer is then repeated, link this movement with the beginning by lowering your hands and placing them again on your shoulders. The third time through this last line is changed as follows:

Grant us peace. Stretch your arms wide open to your sides, with your head lifted and your chest open, ready to receive. Hold this position, feeling the prayer in your body.

All the congregation can do these movements either sitting in the pews or kneeling (if the setting allows). The movements can be adapted for different musical settings.

For a special ending after *"Grant us peace,"* have people turn toward one another and embrace. Recall before doing this the lines from Isaiah about the shepherd gathering and holding the lambs against his breast.

Here is a way to include Isaiah 58. Have a group of people stand apart (either in the aisle or up front) and ask each one to take a body position that helps the person identify with the hungry, or oppressed, or naked, etc. (One approach is to search for these states in yourself and externalize them; another, to notice those you pass on the street.) They hold these positions while another group dances the Lamb of God prayer. On the lines, *"Grant us peace,"* those moving, while stretching out their arms as before, turn their heads toward the others set apart. They then go to them, the "poor," and relate to them in movement, "freeing" them, consoling them. Have lines from Isaiah 58 read in the background while this is happening. Work this out slowly beforehand and experiment with spacing and timing. Everyone need not be helped at the same time. The group should really experience a change, a receiving of love and understanding. A way to end would be with all standing, heads lifted, arms outstretched. Or to repeat a final "Lamb of God . . . " However, another ending might emerge naturally from the work. Let this happen. Music would greatly enhance this section.

"Yes, I Shall Arise"

I have noticed, with dismay but interest, that when I am in a state of indecision, or filled with unexpressed anger, or feeling cutoff from people, that my body is immobile: I cannot move, I am leaden. And if I do move, it is to slowly drag myself along. But then, along the way (through time and sheer grace) a new element enters, and I pick up speed.

I can imagine the prodigal son, immobile in the pit with the hogs, feeling trapped, cutoff, spiritually hitting a dead end. And then, when he came to a decision and said, "Yes, I shall arise!" his energy returning, and his heaving himself to his feet. And then, maybe with alacrity, maybe still with dragging feet, his returning—arising to his father.

Here is a way to explore such a theme of reconciliation with congregations, using the song "Yes, I Shall Arise" by Father Lucien Deiss (*Biblical Hymns and Psalms,* Vol. I, World Library Publications, Inc.).

The congregation sings the entire song. When they come to the final chorus the leader instructs the people to take the following position in their seats: bodies bent over, feet on the floor, heads to their knees, hands hanging down. One should experience in this position a feeling of darkness and stillness and letting go. On the chorus (*"Yes, I shall arise and return to my Father!"*) all, with closed eyes, slowly lift up their backs to a straight position. Repeat the chorus. This time, while slowly opening their eyes, they gradually raise their right hands straight overhead and come to the feet, with a feeling of their whole selves responding to an inner call to life. It's the will from inside that lifts the arm up. This position is held for a few seconds.

"Hear, O Lord" (words and music by Ray Repp, *Hymnal for Young Christians,* F.E.L. Publications, Ltd.) is listed in the hymnal under offertory songs. However, the refrain could be sung and danced as part of a penitential rite or as a response to a reading, as well as other places that seem suitable. The movement is designed for the whole congregation, but perhaps a few people dancing it first would be a good introduction. My own preference is to leave out the verses.

"Hear, O Lord"

First line of the refrain. (Opening position: Palms held at chest level, pressed together, fingers pointing upward.) As the line is sung, slowly raise hands straight upward until arms are stretched overhead. The head follows the upward movement of the hands.

Second line. With a slight impulse open the hands (palms facing upward) and arch the chest backward; keeping the head and chest raised, lower the arms until they are outstretched in front of the chest, slightly above waist level. The gesture is done with the feeling of asking for mercy.

Third line. Stretch the arms out to the sides, bringing the torso back to its normal upright position, but keeping the heart and body very alert, expectant.

Fourth line. Draw the hands back together as in the opening position but not pressed, just held lightly. The head bows at the same time. Hold this position for several seconds in silence, praying.

Note: If any position seems to cause strain instead of prayer, modify. The feeling is more important than the position.

My people, my people

This dance study for Lent is a reflection on the passion and suffering of Jesus. It should also help us focus on our scars and, through identification with Jesus, help us draw closer to this healing love for us.

There is a relation between our wounds and the wounds of Jesus. As Elizabeth Boyden Howes says in her book *Intersection and Beyond,* we all have secret wounds, wounds from childhood, wounds from yesterday's unresolved angers and fears, and these neglected wounds lead us into sin and we wound others. (See "Forgiveness as Wound and Healing," a chapter in *Intersection and Beyond,* San Francisco: Guild for Psychological Studies, 1971.) Psychologists are helping us become more aware of how deeply our bodies register and lock into us these hurts, which we see so clearly manifested in all the knots and tensions we have accumulated.

And so Jesus, too, was wounded by us, and he forgave us.

The core of this study consists of the lines from the Good Friday Reproaches: "My people, my people, what have I done, or in what have I offended thee? Answer me." (If possible, this should be chanted each time it recurs.)

There are two lines of people, of equal number, facing each other. On one side the people assume the role of Jesus and on the other the people are simply themselves (loving, suffering, unwhole, loved by the Lord). Those who represent Jesus stand there, arms outstretched, about chest height, palms facing upward, as if pleading and calling to the person across the way.

As the line is chanted (*"My people . . . "*) the others slowly come forward, each toward a partner, with hands across face, or walking in any body position that is a true expression of sorrow for causing pain to another. By the time the refrain ends, each person has reached a partner and laid his or her head in the hands of "Jesus." "Jesus" simply holds them, or comforts them in an additional way by an embrace.

The line of people then backs away to its original place, and a group that has prepared beforehand a study based on a line from one of the passion narratives or from the Suffering Servant Songs of Isaiah presents it, dancing in the space between the two lines. For the sake of viewers, those in the lines may have to kneel or sit down while the study is going on. After it is completed (around one to three minutes) those in the study leave or take places in the lines, and the sequence (*"My people . . . "*) is repeated. But this time the roles change (the people on the other side are Jesus, and they stretch forth their hands).

The overall shape of the litany study is then: (1) the refrain sung and moved to (one line advancing to the outstretched arms of the other); (2) the line backing away and in the space a study presented, each time to a different passage; (3) the roles changing and the opposite line coming forward on the chant; (4) their backing away and another study, etc.

The studies are prepared beforehand. During the work session the people call to mind their own wounds and sins, reflect and pray. Then each chooses a passage to work on, either alone or with one or two others. They should search for dramatic and movement ideas that reveal the feelings of Jesus, and not try to express every word or idea in the passage. Have someone read the lines before or during the studies.

Here are some suggested passages: Mark 14:34-36; John 19:1-3; John 19:17-18; Isaiah 42:2-4, Isaiah 50:5-7; Isaiah 53:2-5, 7. Please use any others that specially speak to you. The stations of the cross (all fourteen or fewer) could be done this way.

This can be a very powerful experience for those who participate and should be done with silence and solemnity in a relatively dark area lit by candlelight. Again, one needn't be a dancer or actor to participate, but simply be willing to put, with all sincerity, some time and prayer into the project. I have no doubt that beautiful studies will emerge.

I see this litany being suitable for a day of recollection during Lent, for Good Friday, or for any special penitential service, provided the congregation is open to this type of presentation and involvement.

A children's liturgy

In the early Christian communities the newly baptized, to symbolize their new life in Christ, enacted a ritual in which they plunged into the river and emerged on the other side to put on long white robes. This idea was used in the Lower School at the Convent of the Sacred Heart in New York City to help the children understand Lent as a time to go into the "waters" of renewal so as to emerge on Easter a little closer to the newness of life in Christ.

Prior to the liturgy, several children prepared a dance/mime rite of renewal in which they were asked to find in their bodies a posture depicting a particular habit or trait they would like to change in themselves, e.g., fear, selfishness, etc. Or it could be some other negative element in their environment that they would like to see changed—loneliness, sadness, war, hunger, confusion, hatred. After the negative aspect was found in movement, the children then worked out the opposite—peacefulness, love, joy, courage, hope, etc. Then each child in turn enacted the negative feelings, "dove" into the river (which consisted of a long blue scarf, held high, waving above them) and came up on the other side dancing joy, peace, love, and putting on a white mantle. Musical instruments were used to accompany the action: drums for the going down and bells, chimes and stringed instruments for the rising up into new life.—*Contributed by Dorita Beh.*

For home prayer

This may be done alone, with families or in small communities. I am envisioning the following ritual: All are seated on the floor in a circle, hands joined, quietly praying. A candle is in the center, and the rest of the room is darkened. After a few minutes of silence, hands come to the center of the circle, palms facing upward. All chant "Create in me a clean heart, O God." Then the eyes close as the line continues "and put a new and a right spirit within me." As this is chanted, or said, each person slowly raises the hands upward, and then passes them in front of the face and downward toward the heart, feeling the warmth from the hands like a blessing.

Then a psalm is read, the Bible passing around from hand to hand so that everyone can read a few lines in turn. Afterwards all repeat the lines that really struck them in a particular way. Choosing one line, each person meditates on it by praying it with the body, creating a movement image or pattern that helps that person understand the line from the inside. (It helps to softly repeat the words and let the body just respond, almost in a non-thinking way. After a time the body will come up with deeply intuitive responses.) This can be shared with the others or not. Instead of a psalm another passage from scripture could be chosen, such as Mark 10:46-52 (Bartimaeus, the blind beggar), and acted out by the whole group. Bartimaeus cries, "Lord, that I may see!" What do you want to "see" in your life? The acting out can be perceived as a group prayer for each one's self-understanding, the need for inner sight.

Everyone returns to the circle. As a closing, each person goes from one to the next and gently makes the sign of the cross on his or her forehead—a lenten kiss of peace. (What about doing this in church, too?) Each receives the sign in turn from the same person before going on to the next.

Variations on the closing gesture: (1) All bless one another by placing hands on one another's heads. (2) All return to the circle and bless each other simultaneously by stretching arms out to the sides, holding them above the head of the person on either side. Heads are bowed and held in this position for a few minutes. (3) All join hands in the center of the circle, praying in this position, feeling the unity of their common need for God's love and mercy.

EASTER

The following are reflections on the relations between Easter and the desire to dance, some historical accounts of Easter dances in the church, and simple ways to help the body be in harmony with the physical and spiritual well-being implicit in the Easter message.

Dance and Easter

The infusion of spiritual energy galvanizes the body into activity. A few years ago I received a letter from a close friend and former roommate, an atheist, whom I had known to be deeply troubled. I opened it, expecting to read more about her problems. But it began, "Dear beloved sister in Christ . . . Alleluia! I have found the Lord!" Reading it again, with relief and excitement, I shouted delightedly and put on a recording of Bach's *Magnificat*. (I had been working on a dance to this.) Pure joy and exaltation led me to an experience which was spontaneous and powerful. Previously worked out dance steps were but the bare bones for what then became a rich expression of sharing through movement in her resurrection. One bell was struck and all those of like frequency were sounded: "Bring quickly the best robe, and put it on him; and put a ring on his hand, and shoes on his feet; and bring the fatted calf and kill it, and let us eat and make merry; for this my son was dead, and is alive again; he was lost, and is found" (Luke 15:22-24). We know from the older son in the story that they played music and danced.

The wonderful character of Zorba the Greek helps to make dance more understandable and acceptable to many people. The attractiveness of Zorba seems to come from his spontaneous ability to be in touch with his emotions and to express his experience of life in a way that carries him beyond his personal feelings. When no words remain he dances how he feels, and his dance brings life to others.

Sometimes, with a miraculous touch of grace, we can dance when we are heaviest in spirit. Richard Wurmbrand, a Lutheran minister who spent many years in Eastern European prisons, speaks movingly of his new belief in Christ in those circumstances and the incredible joy he experienced which led him to dance in the confinement of his cell. He remembered the whirling dervishes he had seen as a boy; filled with ecstasy, they had called out the name of God as they danced. He remembered David and Miriam in the Bible, the altar boys in Seville, and others who danced when words no longer could give expression to the closeness of God. He describes recalling the words of Jesus, "Blessed are you when men come to hate you, when they exclude you from their company and reproach you and cast out your name as evil on account of the Son of Man. Rejoice in that day and leap for joy." So he began to leap in his cell, to the amazement of his guards. Later, when friends asked him of what use dancing was, he had to explain that it wasn't useful but "a manifestation of joy . . . a holy sacrifice offered before the altar of the Lord." He had "discovered a beauty in Christ." (R. Wurmbrand, *In God's Underground*, Greenwich, Conn.: Fawcett World, 1968.)

Historical references

The sun as the symbol of Christ was the basis of the Renaissance church's custom of tossing a ball or pelota to begin an Easter dance. E. Louis Backman describes pelota as the most characteristic ball game, played even by bishops and archbishops. (*Religious Dances in the Christian Church and in Popular Medicine,* London: Allen and Unwin, 1952.)

With rules dating back to 1396, the game was performed, among other places, in the Cathedral of Auxerres. Men danced a *three step* around the labyrinth inlaid on the floor. Apparently the dean of the cathedral began the Easter hymn, *Victimi Paschali Laudes,* and, with the ball in his left hand, danced to the chant; the priests, holding hands, executed steps around the labyrinth while the dean threw the ball alternately to them. The ceremony was concluded with a feast. Margaret Fisk Taylor comments: "The passing of the ball forward and backward, in the circular dance, in which every dancer also revolved on his own axis, may well have been thought to illustrate the apparent path or dance of the sun in the heavens throughout the year, and so of its 'passion.'" (*A Time to Dance,* Philadelphia: United Church Press, 1967.)

A labyrinth or maze was frequently engraved on church floors to symbolize the road to salvation. There were many labyrinthine dances at Easter to portray Christ leading souls to liberation. (See M.F. Taylor, *A Time to Dance.*)

A wonderful movement image for the sun as a symbol of Christ is contained in Psalm 19 and begins, "The heavens are telling the glory of God; and the firmament proclaims his handiwork." Then we read, "In them he has set a tent for the sun, which comes forth like a bridegroom leaving his chamber, and like a strong man runs its course with joy." What strength and movement—the sun bounding across the heavens in the rapture of love! In the Song of Solomon (2:10-12) we find, "Arise, my love, my fair one, and come away; for lo, the winter is past, the rain is over and gone. The flowers appear on the earth, the time of singing has come . . . " In John 20, Mary Magdalene comes to the tomb early, while it is still dark. Was the sun up when she finally heard her name called and stretched forth her arms to embrace Jesus? (See the *Quem Quaeritis* play described below.)

Another traditional Easter dance, performed in Besancon and other places in France, was the *Bergerette,* described in detail by Margaret Fisk Taylor and E. Louis Backman. On the first day of Easter, the archbishop of Besancon invited the clergy to dinner, after which they danced, either in the cloisters or the nave of the cathedral. The custom continued until the Revolution of 1798. The *Bergerette* seems to have been either a ring or line dance, as hands were held. The hymn to which they danced described the miracle of the resurrection. Paintings of that period also represented the ring dance, with angels and the blessed hand in hand, as, for example, in the works of Fra Angelico and Botticelli. Backman cites many samples of writings on the ring dance and other aspects of sacred dance by Sts. Basil, John Chrysostom, Ambrose, Clement of Alexandria and Gregory of Nazianzen, to name a few.

The Maypole

Springtime, with the bursting of new buds and flowers and fruits, is the natural counterpart to the Easter mystery of death and resurrection. This new life was celebrated by the ancient custom of dancing around a newly blooming tree, which developed into the Maypole dance. Maypoles and Maypole dances go way back in time and were the source of many English country dances. Each tree was thought to have living in it a spirit that was responsible for its fruit. Therefore, each of the tree spirits were propitiated so the tree would bear fruit. When people saw the leaves bursting on a lovely May day, they would join hands and circle joyously around the tree. As the people couldn't carry fruit trees, they began to make poles to represent the trees. Each spring they would decorate the poles with fresh green boughs, searching in the woods the night before to collect branches. (See Violet Alford, *Peeps at English Folk Dances,* London: A. & C. Black, Ltd., 1923.)

In the October 12, 1970 issue of *Time* Magazine, Melvin Maddocks wrote in an article entitled "Rituals—The Revolt Against the Fixed Smile" that the first known attempt to hold a Maypole festival in America was in the spring of 1627, at Plymouth. Thomas Morton erected an eighty-foot pine Maypole and "brewed a barrell of excellent beare," hoping to show the New World how to celebrate. However, Myles Standish and America's "first vice squad" interrupted the revels and Morton was put in stocks and eventually shipped off to England. Maddocks speculates in his article that Maypoles were thought to be dangerous because such festivities were considered to be the works of the devil, the lord of play. Maypole rituals may have suggested feelings and passions that the Pilgrims had come to the New World to escape. Maddocks reviews the empty rituals we now celebrate, such as getting drunk on New Year's Eve or handing out cigars at the birth of a child, and leads us to consider the damage caused by not having allowed the Maypole celebration of 1627 to take place. He says, "Through some hideous gaffe did the anti-Maypolers reject not the devil but one face of God? By being so busy conquering nature that they could not celebrate it, by insisting with prim spiritual pride on reason, did the first Americans cut us all off from the more chaotic but deeper rhythms of life?"

As a child I participated in a Maypole dance. Each pole was decorated with many streamers, and every child was given the end of a streamer to hold. The dance consisted of weaving and circling in and out until the pole was wrapped tighter and tighter by the streamers. Then all joined hands and danced around the pole. There were about twenty poles spread out in a huge park area, each wrapped with colored streamers. It was a wonderful day of unexpected fun and beauty.

Gabe Huck, the editor of *Major Feasts and Seasons,* asked me to give some thought to ways Maypole dances could be revived and adapted for use in Christian celebrations during the weeks of the Easter season. Dancing with the pole and streamers could be prefaced by reading John 15:5: "I am the vine, you are the branches. He who abides in me, and I in him, he it is that bears much fruit, for apart from me you can do nothing." Another approach would be to view the trees as an image of Christ, with all the people (not necessarily only children) moving ever closer to the *center,* weaving in and out of each other's lives. Songs of love and unity could be sung during the dance.

"Make ready for the Christ"

Perhaps because of crowdedness, or lack of awareness, or just physical and spiritual lethargy, there is usually a discrepancy between our bodily posture at prayer in church and our recognition of being in the presence of God (especially on Easter when we celebrate the resurrected body of the Lord!). The posture and physical *presence* of all in church have a bearing on everyone's perception of the resurrection of Christ and his presence in the mass. People go to monasteries to come closer to the holy, which often seems palpable in the very air of the place and in an indefinable way in the *presence* of the monks. Imagine walking into a parish church and seeing everyone intently focused in prayer, all having found their own "still point," all radiating Christ's spirit with body and soul united.

> Make ready for the Christ
> Whose smile, like lightning,
>   sets free the song of everlasting glory
> That now sleeps in your paper-flesh
>   like dynamite!
>   —*Thomas Merton*

The following is an exercise based on these lines. Its intent is to sharpen our sense of the flow of energy and the vitality of movement-response that is waiting to be freed from within us.

Exercise: Bend your torso over, moving into any position. Now clasp your body with your arms (wrapping them around your torso, or holding onto your head, waist, legs—whatever) and exert a strong downward pressure with your arms. When all are in some such inward, downward position, the lines of Merton are read slowly. Each one from this position pushes against the pressure from his or her own hands, so that there is a strong counterforce. This tension is kept while at the same time the torso slowly rises until, on the final word ("dynamite!"), all release their arms and, with a flow of energy, reach outward with arms and torso in a triumphal way.

For a dancer this sequence might lead to an exciting pattern of movement and prayer. But what I hope it will bring the average person is an awareness that when the body is awake the spirit has a chance to catch on fire, and that when the spirit is on fire, the body responds likewise.

The postures of prayer   √   The Easter season, the season of the Lord's resurrection, is a good time to become aware of how we walk, sit, stand, breathe—of how we communicate our faith through our bodies. Whether walking or standing or sitting or kneeling, the goal is to allow energy to flow freely through the body—to become sensitive to the capacity of the body to receive and transmit God's presence and grace.

With this in mind, the following are suggestions to help us be-

come more aware of the power and beauty of the common postures of prayer in church:

Sitting: When sitting in an upright position, take a moment to
check if the spine is straight, if the shoulders are down and open
(not hunched together), legs and chest and neck relaxed, arms
and hands held easily (not holding belongings), perhaps with
palms turned upward as is the custom in some prayer meetings.
Be aware of how your head is held. It makes a difference if the
face is turned upward or downward. Both are "correct" positions.
There is no right or wrong. The idea is to have the position be in
harmony with your inner intention. Lifting the face helps give a
sense of receiving grace and light; lowering the head seems to
help with inner concentration. Notice if your breath is flowing
easily or if it is constrained. If it is constrained, spend a minute
taking deep, long breaths; this will ease the tension (actually think
of breathing out the tension) and prepare you, so to speak, for the
inspiration that will come. Normally the torso should be held with
the spine straight and long, but if you are feeling tired or low,
allow your body to bend over, hands and arms helping in a supportive way, so that the supplicating position of the torso becomes
part of a wordless prayer for strength. One need not maintain a
facade of spiritual well-being. It is important to be in touch with
oneself, and allow the body to help in this inner discernment. If
this seems awkward or impossible during group prayer, find a few
minutes alone beforehand during which you can be in touch with
your feelings and, with the help of the body position, bring them
to consciousness. Offering oneself as one is, in God's light, is
healing.

Standing: When standing one should have the same general
sense of awareness of the body as when sitting: the spine becomes
long and relaxed, yet supportive, and the shoulders and neck muscles are relaxed and open. The body needs to be aligned all the
way from the head to the feet (shoulders in line with the hips and
weight over the balls of the feet) for real comfort free from strain.
Think of the building blocks of a child. When they are stacked
one above the other, some forward, some back, they easily fall
over. The body compensates for lack of alignment with muscle
tension and strain, but this use of energy is self-defeating. The
weight should be aligned to avoid such tension. To stand in ease
allows the spirit to flow more smoothly. To "stand before the

Lord" will have new meaning and beauty when the body and spirit are in harmony.

Bowing: Think of the bow as a melting and yielding of the spirit. Begin with lowering the head and then bit by bit bend the torso forward, feeling the spine move one vertebra after the other. (This image is often used in dance classes to achieve a smooth, sequential flow of movement.) Be aware that the hands and arms, in whatever position they are, are part of the prayer. Experiment at home with all the different ways the arms can be held, and sense what each position is expressing. When the bow is completed, unfold the spine in the same sequential manner, starting with the lowest part of the spine that is bent forward and uncurling into a straight position, head lifting last.

Genuflecting: This can be a movement of great beauty when the flow of the arm gesture and lowering of the torso are completed at the same time. The unity of the movement—all parts moving in rhythm and harmony and coming to rest at the same time in the kneeling position—becomes a form suitable for the spirit's offering of itself. (It has a chance to say: "I dedicate myself, and here I am.") To genuflect with this quality one has to bend the knee very slowly so that the many movements that the hand has to make can be done in an unhurried way. One could count this: (1) hand to forehead, (2) to heart, (3) to left shoulder, (4) to right shoulder, and again, (1) arm to side and knee touching floor. Pause a moment to "pray" this position of the body. Then slowly rise.

Walking: "I walk before the Lord in the land of the living" (Psalm 116:9). The psalmist describes what we have been striving toward: to walk, sit, stand, pray in the presence of the Lord. When walking (to receive communion, to present the gifts, to collect the offering) do not think of your body as a hulk of matter that simply gets you somewhere, but as a beautiful servant of your inner person (closer than a servant—your "right arm"— even your very self). Walking forward toward the altar is an opportunity to offer yourself, just as you are, without apologies (as it seems when shoulders are hunched over and chests are caved in and leaning backward). We don't have to apologize for existing before God, our loving Creator, or anyone else. Walk forward as if "leading with the heart," which means holding the chest open, carrying your weight forward, making each step positive, and moving with love. Focusing on the body in this way, as a temple of the Holy Spirit, will not be distracting from the inner attention on communicating with the Lord.

Space and focus: Understanding how the use of space and focus affects a congregation is very important. There is a heightened sense of participation and communication when people see faces, instead of backs, in front of or around them. In the communion line it is only the strong *common* inner focus that makes up for the sense of separateness and child-like discipline generated by long lines with people's backs to one another. Paradoxically, many people feel communion to be much richer and more personal when they are aware of the rest of the community. This is easily managed with small groups that can be gathered around the altar. At New York University chapel there are too many people at Sunday mass to all gather in the sanctuary area. However, a sizable group of people elect to stay in the sanctuary after the presentation of the gifts. Their presence around the altar gives a sense of community to those coming up for communion. Also, the closer one is spacially to the central action or mystery, the more awake one is; this new awareness is communicated to others farther away by a subtle change in stance and energy. The common arrangement of setting up different stations, usually in a semi-circle behind the altar, also helps give the sense of participating with others in this personal act, particularly when there are many lines that converge from different directions. All this should be done slowly. It takes time to experience the mysterious interweaving of our lives.

Easter is a time for all to dance, and it is also a time to invite trained dancers to perform special dances of the resurrection. In planning dance for the liturgies, decide on the mood you want to help create. Do you want to emphasize the exultation of Easter, or have a joyous folksy celebration, or one that imparts deep peace? Talk this over with the dancers in the community and invite them to meet with the music and liturgy committees so that the dance is coordinated with the rest of the liturgy. Then, too, the dance director can plan simple gestures for all to do, either as part of the dance or at another point in the liturgy. Spontaneous or taught circle dances at the close of mass (to songs

The moods of Easter

such as "Lord of the Dance") are particularly suitable for purely joyous celebrations and masses for young people, but would not be appropriate for a mood of great solemnity. I saw an exception to this one Easter, however, when everyone, led by the presider, burst out into spontaneous dancing to Alexander Peloquin's "All the Ends of the Earth." In that community enough people were accustomed to spontaneity so that the mood of exultation did not deteriorate during the improvisation but actually brought the mass to a wonderful climax.

Glory to God

One Easter three of us danced the Glory to God as part of the vigil service at Mary Reparatrix Convent in New York City. This dance was composed and performed by Kateri Terns, Claudet Gazet and myself.

We distributed beforehand all kinds of bells which were rung right before the start and all during the Glory to God, as is usual for an Easter service. It would be lovely to hear bells ringing to announce the Glory to God on other festive days. They certainly quicken the energy of dancers and, I suspect, of everyone else as well.

This description for three dancers gives the idea for the basic form, but the dance can be done by any number of people with the necessary spacial adjustments. The suggestions can also be adapted to varying tempos and melodies. We used a simple chant. Though the dance is very simple, it should be directed by someone with some dance background or feeling for movement qualities.

Glory to God in the highest. Three dancers, starting from different points in the church, joyously run to the center (in front of the altar), lifting up their arms as they do so. They meet and form a small circle, heads, chests, and arms uplifted.

and peace to his people on earth. The dancers first wish each other peace. They slowly and gently lower their arms past one another's head and shoulders, looking at each other. Then they step backward and open up the circle to form a line, all facing front, smoothly changing their arms so that their hands are extended forward, in greeting to everyone, palms facing upward, about waist height. Their feet are together. The center person is slightly forward.

Lord God, heavenly King, almighty God and Father. Each person, keeping the right foot where it is, shifts weight backward onto the left foot, bending the left knee. At the same time each slowly turns the palms face downward and raises the arms above the head with a feeling of awe and reverence. The head is lowered between the arms and the gaze is downward.

we worship you. The dancer to the left of the middle person comes forward and kneels, facing sideways (to the right). Arms are curved outward, head lowered, one knee to the floor, back rounded over—the body conveying a feeling of adoration.

we give you thanks. The dancer to the right of the middle person steps forward, taking a position in back of the first dancer to move, but facing in the opposite direction (i.e., left), and slightly to the right of the middle dancer (now in the back). This dancer maintains an in between height, with kneels slightly bent, body rounded over, arms expressing thanks in whatever way feels best.

we praise you for your glory. The middle dancer straightens up, bringing the feet together, stretching one arm upward, palm facing outward, and lowering the other arm so that it is rounded in front (about waist high), palm facing upward.

Note: As you can see, in this last section each dancer has one phrase on which to move and express by his or her position a response to the words. Only one dancer is moving at a time.

Lord Jesus Christ, only Son of the Father, Lord God, Lamb of God. All three dancers lower their arms and stand facing front as before, middle person slightly forward. (This is a transition movement allowing the side two dancers to get back to their straight line.) They then bend to the right in unison and extend their right arms sideways and overhead, with a long reaching movement. This blends into the next sequence.

you take away the sin of the world. All bend to the left while their right arms curve overhead and their left arms fold in front of their bodies. They hold this left side bend and left arm position and lower their right arms further down across their faces while turning their heads to the right and upward. This head gesture initiates a slow turning of the whole body to the right. (The arm gesture, passing in front of the face, is done with a feeling of washing away sin or shame or tears, or simply with a feeling of looking to the Lord.)

have mercy on us. All continue turning till they are facing the altar with their backs to the congregation. They then drop to their right knees, extending their arms upward as they lower themselves. The movement has strength in the pull of the opposition (arms upward, body downward). Heads are lifted in a cry for mercy.

you are seated at the right hand of the Father. All rise and repeat the previous movement (bending to the left with the right arm stretching overhead to the left and across the face and down, and the left arm held curved in front of the body at about hip height). While rising all are also turning to the right until they are again facing front. (This movement will melt into the following one.)

receive our prayer. All face each other in a small circle with palms facing upward, held about waist high. Everyone's head slowly lifts up and the hands also begin to rise upward, to a small degree, so that there is a feeling of living, rising prayer.

For you alone are the Holy One. All execute a side lunge to the right (weight on the right leg, right knee bent and left leg straight) with bodies facing front. The direction of the lunge is to the right and diagonally between straight side and back, so that the three dancers are on an angle to the front (upstage right corner). Arms are held at the sides, straight and close to the body in a parallel line, and the head is turned to the left and upward. There should be a feeling of awe in the movement and a sense of the presence of God in all directions as the body shifts into the different positions in the next two movements.

you alone are the Lord. Keeping the body and arms as still as possible, all shift their weight to the left leg (reversing the lunge) and turn their heads to the right and upward.

you alone are the Most High. Holding the weight in their left legs, all rotate their bodies so that they are in a back lunge position. The body is way back in this position, chest and face lifted upward.

Jesus Christ. All shift their weight forward (still keeping their backs and chests lifted) onto their right legs, in a forward lunge position, and raise their arms upward with a feeling of praise.

with the Holy Spirit. All back away with small running steps (a "breath run"), adjusting to form a small circle. Arms are raised to the sides.

in the glory of God the Father. All run together to the center of the circle, arms uplifted as in the beginning of the dance.

Amen. As an ending and as a way of moving gracefully out of sight, all walk backward, making the circle ever wider, turning slightly from side to side. The arms are in an extended position, forward and up, and slightly bent to avoid stiffness and to allow a feeling of wonder and an ever-fresh response to God's glory. The arms open with the legs on each backward step, head and body turning slightly in the same direction.

Quem Quaeritis?

This ancient play, traditionally performed on Easter morning, was the first piece of scripture to have been dramatized in the liturgical service. Our whole tradition of Western drama grew from this simple and vital source. The *Quem Quaeritis* play was really the fountainhead.

This simple form of the ancient play still works its enchantment in telling the good news:

1. The three women, with bowed heads and gestures of mourning, weave their way down the aisle to the altar, saying to one another,
   "Who will roll the stone for us?"
   "Who will roll away the stone?"

2. At the altar, the angel suddenly appears. The women cry out and fall back, covering their faces. The angel says,
   "Don't be afraid.
   Whom are you looking for?"

3. The women rise and call,
   "Where is Jesus,
   The man who was crucified?"

4. The angel indicates the empty tomb: "He isn't here!" He raises his arms slowly and majestically: "As he said, he has risen!" He gestures toward the congregation: "Now go and tell everybody!"

5. The women turn and call,
   "Peter! Andrew! James! John!
   Everyone! Hurry up! Come to the tomb!"

They repeat this, flying down the steps to the aisle. Then, dancing and spinning in joy, they cry out to people in each pew such phrases as "Jesus is risen!" "The tomb! It's empty!" "Jesus is alive!" "Hurry, come and see!" "Run and tell everyone!"

91

6. When they reach the back of the church, the disciples, and anyone else who wants to join in, run and skip and cartwheel forward, with ringing and jingling bells. Some call out: "Oh, Hallelujah! Jesus is risen!" Simultaneously, others cry: "Jesus is risen? I can't believe it!" Others, "Christ is alive! How can it be?" All converge at the altar, point out "the empty tomb" to each other, then are joined by the choir in leading the congregation in a favorite hymn of resurrection.

This could open the service, it could be the gospel reading of the day, or it could be the day's homily. May the sacred exuberance of Easter fill you to the tips of your toes! —*Nick Hodsdon*

Dancing to Scripture

I believe that there is in all congregations, no matter how seemingly passive, an unexpressed, often unperceived but real expectation and yearning to be led into the kingdom of heaven—a desire to have some of God's love and beauty seep through, and crash through, our heaviness and dullness and wake us to a deep and wonderful reality. I know I go to liturgy to learn about and, hopefully, to dwell in this special life, and I learn through my head, my heart and my senses.

Scriptures can be presented in such a way that our whole selves become engrossed in this learning about the kingdom. (How often is only our mind dimly engaged!) It is possible to see and feel and understand more of the depth and beauty of the scriptures when they are visualized for us in their presentations, "incarnated," as it were, through bodily participation. When our body and our senses are involved, our spirit becomes more involved, for we are a totality. In ordinary life we are always watching "bodies" move about their daily business. Our search is for the spiritual dimensions of normal activity and perceptions.

The psalm of the day can be danced, with simple gestures given to the congregation for their response. Here is a detailed description, using Psalm 24, of this approach. It involves preparation beforehand by two readers and three groups of participants: a) a group responsible for the main movements; b) a group responsible for learning and teaching the congregation's part; c) a group to provide music (improvising with simple rhythm instruments of all varieties).

The Rehearsal. Those present divide into three sections: the musicians sit by the side; the dancers group together in the center, and those learning the congregation's part face them, sitting, as if in the pews. One reader is up in front, as if by the lectern, and

Learning and liturgy

Psalm 24

the other (second reader) as if in back of the church.

All read the psalm together to familiarize themselves with the form and the meaning.

The musicians experiment with the different sounds and rhythms they can produce and work out a loose plan of what qualities or effects they want for the various parts of the psalm. (At one workshop we used woodblocks, bells, kalimba, flex-a-tone, drum, tambourine and harmonica.) The players must be sensitive to the words, the timing of the dance movements, and the sounds of the other instruments. Those who have more training can provide the core melodies and rhythms around which others can work.

FIRST READER:
The earth is the Lord's and the fullness thereof. The dancers, grouped in the center (two or three lines of three or four people each), hold their hands cupped in front of them, fingers pointing upward. They slowly separate their hands as if the round ball of the earth were expanding before their eyes. (All movements are only suggestions for beginning or nondancers and can be added to and enriched in many ways without breaking the movement and response form.)

the world and those who dwell therein. With a slight impulse, curving their torsos forward, they draw in their fingertips toward the center of their chests (as if the world were within them), then open their hands slowly outward while straightening their backs and take hold of the hands of the persons on either side of them.

for he has founded it upon the seas, and established it upon the rivers. All take a few running steps forward, raising their hands and lifting their chests (a "breath run") and then take a few steps backward, torsos bending forward, arms moving backward. The quality is like the tide of an ocean—in and out—with a peak (the forward movement) and an ebb.

SECOND READER:
Who shall ascend the hill of the Lord? Musicians stop. The dancers are still. The congregation, seated, gesture forward with their right hands, toward the dancers, as if the words were coming from them. (This is done with strength and fullness, while the reader is saying the line.)

And who shall stand in his holy place? The congregation withdraw their right hands to cover their faces with both hands (palms facing out). The faces are turned away, as if averted from the holy presence of the Lord. (Hands slowly lower during the next few lines.)

FIRST READER:
He who has clean hands and a pure heart, who does not lift up his soul to what is false, and does not swear deceitfully. (Musicians play softly.) The dancers, almost in slow motion (avoiding a salute-like quality), move their hands in front of their hearts and upward ending with their right hands held up, palms facing out, and left hands over the heart area, palms facing in.

He will receive blessing from the Lord. Dancers lift up their faces and, moving left hands up to meet right hands, lower both hands a few inches in front of their faces and downward, as if receiving blessing through their palms.

and vindication from the God of his salvation. Both hands stop their descent and hold together with firmness in front of the torso, one hand in front of the other.

Such is the generation of those who seek him. With small steps, all make a complete turn in place to the right and, while doing so, raise their hands, still pressed together, in front of their faces. They stop, facing the congregation.

who seek the face of the God of Jacob. Palms slowly separate sideways and then downwards, revealing each dancer's face, which is gazing outward with stillness and intensity.

(Musicians pick up in volume and rhythm and then the first reader continues:)

Lift up your heads, O gates! / and be lifted up, O ancient doors! / that the King of glory may come in. All dancers sharply raise faces upward. On the second line they raise hands to shoulder level (with an accent—movement is percussive in contrast to the preceding slow, reflective motions) and then upward, in a V shape. (Face is still uplifted.) On the third line they step forward in unison, clapping hands on "King" and on "glory," ending with arms upraised. (The clap is performed in a large way, arms extending outward after each clap.)

SECOND READER:
(Musicians stop.)

Who is the King of glory? The congregation stand and once again reach out with their right hands toward the dancers.

FIRST READER:
The Lord, strong and mighty, the Lord, mighty in battle!
(Congregation and dancers move together.) All cross arms in front of chest and grasp the hands of the persons on either side.

(Musicians pick up in volume and rhythm and then the first reader continues:)

Lift up your heads, O gates! and be lifted up, O ancient doors! that the King of glory may come in. Congregation and dancers both do the same movements that were described above for the dancers. (The congregation clap without moving forward.)

SECOND READER:
(Musicians stop.)

Who is this King of glory? Dancers and congregation stand perfectly still, holding last position.

FIRST AND SECOND READERS:
The Lord of hosts, he is the King of glory! Dancers and congregation make a complete turn in place, circling to the right, with a feeling of praise running through their upturned faces and raised arms. They end facing each other. All slowly lower arms. (On one occasion a few, beautiful sustained notes were played on the harmonica at this point, closing the psalm with a sense of mystery and eternity.)

Psalm 36

How precious is thy steadfast love, O God / The children of men take refuge in the shadow of thy wings. / They feast on the abundance of thy house, / and thou givest them drink from the river of thy delights. / For with thee is the fountain of life; / in thy light do we see light. —Psalm 36:7-9

This is a psalm-prayer in movement, to be done in pairs by any even number of people. Practice in a peaceful atmosphere so that it can be explored slowly. It could be done just as a prayer exercise, or incorporated in a liturgy as one of the readings.

How precious is thy steadfast love, O God! Take partners and spread out around the room. One member of each pair begins by kneeling, or sitting back on his heels, body bent over; the other begins by standing, facing him. Hold this position while the first line is slowly read. Then in response, the person kneeling raises his back and lifts up his hands, palms upward, as the standing person (a "God figure" of love) bends forward and lowers his hands, palms downward, till they meet the upraised hands of his partner. This is done very slowly, so that the meeting of the hands becomes a meaningful moment.

The children of men take refuge in the shadow of thy wings. While the line is read, the lower person in each set rises to his knees and each couple then slowly embraces, folding arms around one another, each one in his own way.

They feast on the abundance of thy house. The "God figure" helps the kneeling person to rise, then grasps with the right hand the partner's left hand and steps backward in a small circle, as the partner walks forward. The "God figure" leads the other gently around, gestures with the free hand as if showing the "house"—the river of delights. Think of it as a thanksgiving in movement for God's bounty.

and thou givest them drink from the river of thy delights. The "God figure" bends down as if scooping imaginary water and, rising, passes it to his partner who with cupped hands and swaying body accepts it in a variety of ways (as if drinking deeply, or bathing under a fountain, etc.). This passing and receiving can be done a number of times.

For with thee is the fountain of life. Both people stop gradually and come to a standing position facing one another, a few feet apart. Each one's hands are placed a few inches in front of his face, palms facing inward.

in thy light do we see light. All slowly separate their hands as if parting a curtain and look at their partners face to face, receiving "light" from one another. This position is held for a few seconds.

Note: This is simply an outline for a movement meditation. Each couple must make it its own. If possible, go over the text beforehand and have someone lead some movement warm-ups. (One preliminary way would be to call out key words in the psalm such as precious, refuge, abundance, light, etc., and invite every-body to find movements in response.) It is also helpful to play meditative music during the study, such as *Music for Zen Meditation,* Verve V6-8634.

Psalm 115 (116)

This dance is for congregational use at a liturgy emphasizing trust and hope. It is based on the arrangement for singing according the psalmody of Joseph Gelineau found in *Twenty-four Psalms and a Canticle,* published by the Gregorian Institute of America.

I trusted even when I said: "I am sorely afflicted." All in congregation, while sitting in pews, raise arms and eyes slowly, timing the gesture with the phrasing of the music. (Chant in a calm, meditative way.) Think of the upward movement of the arms as a call to God, reaching through time and space.

and when I said in my alarm: "No man can be trusted." All slowly lower arms and grasp neighbors' hands.

How can I repay the Lord for his goodness to me? A few peo-ple will have gathered in the back of the church beforehand. They now process slowly down the aisle, each carrying one gift to be placed later on the altar. The person in front carries the chalice.

The cup of salvation I will raise; I will call on the Lord's name. All pause. (They should be midway down the aisle.) The leader slowly lifts up the chalice (holding it in both hands, eyes raised) and then the others raise their gifts.

Your servant, Lord, your servant am I; you have loosened my bonds. All turn in place very slowly, keeping gifts still lifted high for all to see.

A thanksgiving sacrifice I make, I will call on the Lord's name. Resume walking to the altar (a little more joyfully) and place the gifts on the altar (or hand to the priest) and stand in a semicircle in front of the altar.

My vows to the Lord I will fulfill before all his people. All bow slowly, facing altar, and then rise, lifting up arms. The priest lifts up his arms and head in a movement of dedication to the Lord while the others are bowing, holding his arms up till they join him in the same movement.

in the courts of the house of the Lord. All in front of the altar make one complete turn in place, keeping body and arms still lifted.

in your midst, O Jerusalem. Those by the altar join hands, with arms raised. At the same time all those in the pews, still holding their neighbors' hands, raise their arms too. Pause in unity.

The Emmaus story

The following is a description of a way of dramatizing the Emmaus story, which can be done by quite a large number of people and doesn't take more than one good rehearsal. Each time it has been done it has been a deeply meaningful experience for all those present; I see it as an example of dance, drama and scripture working together. It was first conceived as part of an Institute for the Study of Religious Education and Service at Boston College. About thirty people performed it, though finally the whole congregation was involved. It would be suitable for sometime soon after Easter.

The idea emerged from the song "All Along the Way" from Weston Priory's album, *Listen:*

> All, all along the way, / when we had thought all our hopes had died, / suddenly a stranger came by and asked us why we looked so sadly, / "Have you not heard of the terrible things that happened these past days?"

> In the breaking of the bread we recognized who he really was. / We could see life in a new way and believe that he had risen. / All he had said to us now had real meaning, alive in wonder.

> Now, now we know for sure there is a way of opening to life, / to receive a stranger's vision, / hidden purpose of his presence to live on in us, / and be born again, yes, born again.

The dancers are dispersed throughout the congregation. They rise in silence, a few seconds before the guitarist begins to softly sing, *"All, all along the way . . . "* Their bodies are in positions of great sadness and dejection, burdened with sorrow. They move slowly toward the center (maintaining their body positions), stopping in front of and to the sides of the altar, but keeping a clear space in the middle. At the same time the priest, or whoever will be portraying Jesus, is walking from another direction, and ends up, unnoticed, also by the altar. The guitarist stops after

101

"why we looked so sadly," and the person in the role of Jesus says aloud words like, "Why are you so sad? What are you talking about?"

Then the guitarist continues singing, *"Have you not heard of the terrible things that happened these past days?"* While he sings this a choreographed action takes place. Four people who have worked out beforehand body positions that convey some aspect of Jesus' agony will move, one by one, into the cleared center space, while the rest of the group holds utterly still, bodies bent over in dejection.

The first person, moving on the words *"Have you not heard of,"* crouches in a low position toward the front, perhaps in a position representing one of the times Jesus fell as he was carrying the cross. The second person moves on *"the terrible things"* and takes a position upstage of the first, though slightly on a diagonal for visibility. He maintains this at a slightly higher level than the first. The third person moves on *"happened these"* and is again slightly higher in body position, also in agony and diagonally behind the second person. The fourth person moves into place on *"past days"* and takes the last position which is full height, though twisted as if crucified, and furthest upstage.

All in all it will look like four steps to the crucifixion, portraying in a visible way the "terrible things that happened these past days." The singer stops and there is complete silence and stillness as this final tableau is allowed to sink in.

Then Jesus, moving among all the disciples, says the line from the scriptures, "O foolish men, and slow of heart to believe all that the prophets have spoken!" (Luke 24:25) and then, improvising, continues with words of encouragement and instruction. As he is speaking, all up front gradually relax their body positions, and slowly turn their heads toward him in belief and disbelief, encouraged by his presence.

The guitarist continues with the *second stanza.* While this is sung, Jesus moves toward the altar and in a silent and deeply meaningful way, "breaks the bread." This could be done by bending his torso forward, holding his hands close to his heart, as if breaking the bread were breaking his own self, and then slowly straightening up and drawing his hands apart, as if holding the two halves of bread. All the disciples really change during this. Their faces break out in wonder and they move closer and closer to him (somewhat in slow motion, as there is not much "action" but a lot of inner movement to be conveyed), perhaps reaching toward him with their hands.

As the third and last stanza is sung, *"Now, now we know for sure . . . "* until the end of the song, the disciples move among the congregation and draw people with them up to the altar, including as many as possible. Along the way some might form little circles, dancing quietly for joy. The presentation ends with many people in the sanctuary area, arms upraised, praising the risen Lord, or simply rejoicing that he is in their midst. (At this point, the priest who was "Jesus" in Boston just naturally moved behind the altar and continued with the liturgy.)

"Are Not Our Hearts," by Father Carey Landry, could be danced as a conclusion to a liturgy using the Emmaus reading, or as a simple dance of prayer and praise for any occasion. It can be done by a small or large number of people. There is no opening formation, just an informal grouping of people in a cleared area.

"Are Not Our Hearts"

Are not our hearts burning within us? / Are not our hearts lighted with fire? All turn to the nearest person and take right hands in a loving clasp. On the first line one person draws the hand of the other, with his own, to his chest, holding it over his heart. On the second line the other person draws her hand, still clasped with her partner's to her own heart. (It's as if each one says to the other, "See, my heart is on fire. I want you to share my love and excitement.")

Jesus is with us, is risen, is with us, / Jesus is risen, is with us today. All hold right hands with their partners, shoulder height, and move in a clockwise direction, making a circle. The step for this part is like a waltz step, a *down, up, up; down, up, up.* Take four of these in one direction and then reverse your direction on the second line by quickly changing hands (so that left hands are now held) and circle in a counterclockwise direction with four more waltz steps (*down, up, up; down, up, up,* (or) think, *right, left, right; left, right, left,* etc.). The outside arms are held high, and the body leans outward, away from the partner.

Jesus is the Lord, / Jesus is the Lord. All separate, slow down from the spinning momentum, walk slowly around, in any direction, with raised arms, uplifted face, praising and adoring the Lord.

103

On the second line everyone reverently bows (slowly lowering their arms, genuflecting, curving their torsos over).

Upon straightening up, each turns to a new partner and begins again.

Note: It would be best if the song were sung live and repeated at least four times.

Matthew 6:25-33

Here is a simple example of "moving" into the scripture that was presented one summer as part of a workshop on dance and prayer at the Paulist Center in Boston. It turned out to be quite "moving" and I hope you have a chance to try it.

The text chosen was Matthew 6:25-33. After a process of discussing the passage, pooling ideas, and trial and error, a simple approach was arrived at and presented. (A core group of six worked it out and taught it to about twenty-five people who did it for the congregation as the gospel reading.) The people at the Paulist Center are quite used to scripture being presented in a variety of ways. For this special liturgy we taught them the Our Father dance and another movement prayer so that they were also participating with their bodies.

The twenty-five people were dispersed throughout the chapel. They rose in silence when it was time for the gospel and walked to the sanctuary. All moved in different ways, expressing through their walk and in their bodies an anxiety they felt in their own lives. Arriving at any place around the altar, everyone crouched or stood in some manner filled with tension, body held almost rigid by the conflicting forces. (Literally so—one arm reaching in one direction, another pulling against it, torso twisted, etc.)

The priest (or deacon, as in this instance) quietly walked into view and, looking at them softly, said, "Therefore I tell you, do not be anxious about your life, what you shall eat or what you shall drink, nor about your body, what you shall put on. Is not life more than food, and the body more than clothing?" On *"Look at the birds of the air"* to the end of the passage, he moved slowly and continuously among them, bending down and saying the lines in an individual and personal way—helping first this one to his feet and then looking into the eyes of that one, or pointing out the beautiful world around to another.

Each person that he touched slowly relaxed his or her position, with a feeling of gratitude and release, and rose and joined some-one else; they embraced, or circled around, and gradually, in twos and threes, moved off to their seats. By the last line (*"But seek first his kingdom and his righteousness, and all these things shall be yours as well"*), the deacon was alone by the altar and the others back in their seats or on their way. He directed this line to the whole congregation. Then there was a time of silence before the liturgy moved on.

What will be most meaningful and convey the most learning is (1) the loving, simple way the priest or deacon, as from the heart of Christ, utters and speaks with his body the healing words as he moves about, and (2) the truth of the body positions of tension and anxiety and then their release from that state. No dance training is necessary. What is needed is to experiment beforehand with bodily tensions and releases so as not to "pose" in what *seems* to be a distressful position. Each person has to really find out and express what his or her body already knows of tension and worry (which will reveal a lot to oneself) to experience fully the release and help to be received.

May the words and movements of the Lord bring life!

"Mary . . . sat at the Lord's feet and listened to his teaching. But Martha was distracted with much serving . . . " (Luke 10: 39-40).

Mary and Martha

One summer, Jalabala Vaidya and Gopal Sharman of the Akshara Theatre of India were invited to teach the *katha* form of Hindu religious drama for the Jesuit Institute of the Arts held in New York City, and help us adapt the form to Western scrip-ture. (*Katha* simply means "story.") This form of theater has exciting possibilities for presenting the gospels in a new and force-ful way in the liturgy, and also for workshops and individual study on prayer and scripture. It was a fascinating experience, and I will describe a few of the steps involved, as well as a *katha* I designed, which I hope will make it possible for you to try to create your own, adapting the form to your own needs, liturgical or otherwise.

Here are the steps in what is essentially a personal dramatization of a typical human conflict.

1. You are the actor, playing all the essential roles. You start

in the audience or congregation, dressed like everyone else (maybe wearing a shawl to cover anything special you may be wearing for later in the action). You present your dilemma: It can be a question of our time—be it of boredom with life, of loveless duty, how to live one's life in this situation, etc.

2. You approach the stage, or sanctuary, and receive an intimation of help through divine guidance—a whisper of an answer from one who found freedom from the limitations of time and human knowledge. For example, this could be words from a saint, or from the Holy Spirit (represented by a candle or other symbol).

3. Going further, you stop in front of the altar, or a symbol representing God (a crucifix, candle, icon, etc.) and pray for aid, asking to be emptied, divested of your limited personality, and to be imbued with the presence and cares of the characters you are about to portray, and whose stories are to be told. Then you completely prostrate yourself in front of the altar (or God-figure) and hold this position long enough for the prayer to be real.

4. Rising, you go to where the Bible or other sacred book has been placed and become the storyteller.

5. After reading a few lines you close the book and enter into the story, becoming the characters.

The *katha* which I designed is based on the account of Mary and Martha. It follows the steps given above. (My sister, upon seeing it, exclaimed that she wanted to try it. She instinctively felt that if she could experience in her own body the frantic, hurrying actions of a Martha, in contrast to the slow, contemplative ones of a Mary, she could become aware of when in real life she became a Martha and hopefully be able to stand back and laugh at herself. The body does have a kinesthetic memory.)

1. *The conflict:* I jumped out of my seat crying out, "I can't sit still! Too much to do! Who has time to pray?" and began to move with the words, "Time, time, time. I'm ripped in all directions. Yes, do this; no, do that! Be here! Be there! Be where? All night long I think of things to do. Work, work, work! I'm swirling. Trapped in a net. Isn't this important? Isn't that important? For whom? For me? My own merry-go-round? So who can help me? Is there no way out?" Finally I cried, "Still me!" and collapsed (in front of the candle that I chose to represent the Holy Spirit).

2. *Intimation of help:* The lines from Matthew 11:28-30 were

whispered offstage: "Come to me, all who labor and are heavy laden, and I will give you rest. Take my yoke upon you, and learn from me; for I am gentle and lowly in heart, and you will find rest for your souls. For my yoke is easy, and my burden is light." I arose and slowly walked to the crucifix.

3. *The prayer:* Bowing in front of the crucifix, I spoke aloud, asking the Lord to make my body and spirit a channel to express the beauty and truth of his word. I then prostrated myself.

4. *The storyteller:* Rising, I opened the Bible to Luke 10:38 and read: "Now as they went on their way, he entered a village; and a woman named Martha received him into her house. And she had a sister called Mary, who sat at the Lord's feet and listened to his teaching. But Martha was distracted with much serving . . . "

5. *The story:* Closing the Bible, I began the dance. I used gentle Japanese Koto music when I was dancing Mary. The movements were all in slow motion, enabling me to really pray, holding the Lord in my heart. After about a minute the music increased in tempo and I jumped up and became Martha, shouting, "Someone's got to set the table!" I proceeded to "set the table," using exaggerated motions, throwing imaginary things around, finally becoming so distraught that I ripped apart a flower that was in a bowl on the altar. At this point I stopped and screamed, "Lord, do you not care that my sister has left me to serve alone? Tell her then to help me!" and crouched into a tight ball. I turned and slowly relaxed my body as someone softly read the concluding lines: "Martha, Martha, you are anxious and troubled about many things; one thing is needful. Mary has chosen the good portion, which shall not be taken away from her." Slowly rising, coming to myself, I "chose the good portion," symbolized by reaching for the remaining flowers and handing them out, softly repeating the lines, "The good portion. Choose the good portion . . . "

I find the immediate value of the scriptures so much more apparent when I get in touch with how they relate to an existential problem in my own life. The Mary-Martha conflict of feeling trapped by duties with "no time" to pray was very real to me, and the words and actions of the drama came pouring out.

Work on your own problem, or suggest this approach to a dance-drama group in your church. The *katha* was taught to us as a form for a solo performer. However, we were given permission to experiment, and group *kathas* were presented during a week's workshop on dance and prayer held at St. Andrew's Priory, Valyermo, California. They met with great success. The themes ranged from how to live with certainty in a world that is changing (Jesus in the boat in the storm was portrayed), to how to live with a feeling of barrenness (the faith of Hannah from the First Book of Samuel was portrayed), to how to become a "new" person, not self-centered (the prodigal son was the conclusion).

The first step is to meditate on the basic problem and write out the script; then search the scriptures for an answer. The *katha* form, with its conflict-answer-prayer structure is inherently dramatic and religious, making it ideal for presentation in a worship service.

Ephesians 3

In a recent book by Maria-Gabriele Wosien entitled *Sacred Dance, Encounter with the Gods* (New York: Avon, 1974), there is a picture of an old man with a child in front of him. Both are facing outward. The old man has his arms wrapped around the child and his hands are in front of the child's hands. With palms pressed together, fingers straight, he holds a prayer position. The child's hands are held in the same way. The man's head is tilted slightly downward and he seems to be teaching the child to pray by molding the child's body and hands with his own. They share the intimacy of love and prayer.

This image of teaching another to pray through one's own body was the inspiration for the following dance-prayer to my own paraphrase of the text of Ephesians 3:14-20. It can be shared with members of a family or by any two people, during informal prayers or as a dance-prayer to accompany the reading in a liturgy.

Instructions: Work with a partner, one person taking the role of the child, the other that of the father.

Both start in a standing position. The father is close in back of the child, arms at his sides.

This, then, is what I pray. The father wraps his arms around the child and folds the latter's hands into the prayer position (palms together, fingertips pointing outward). His hands are in the same position, over the child's hands.

kneeling before the Father, from whom every family, whether spiritual or natural takes its name. The father opens the child's hands (his right hand directing the child's right hand, his left the

108

child's left) and places the child's arms to his sides, while at the same time bowing. Both lower to their right knees. Their legs won't tangle if the father is in back and slightly to the side of the child. They hold this kneeling position with torsos slightly bent forward until the end of the line.

Out of his infinite glory. The father takes the child's hands and raises them to the child's shoulders as both torsos straighten. With a slight impulse, he raises the hands overhead in a wide V position (glory). Both lift their heads upward.

may he give you the power through his Spirit. Hands unclasp, but the raised up position is held. This pause is to allow time to *receive* the Spirit.

for your hidden self to grow strong. The father lowers his arms, and with the child's hands in his, places them over the child's heart. Their torsos are curved forward.

so that Christ may live in your hearts through faith. The father opens the child's hands so that the palms face outward, and slowly directs his arms forward and open, as if teaching the child to open himself to others. It is as if the movement expresses one's daring to live in faith with Christ.

and then, planted in love and built on love. The father turns the child toward him. It works easily if the child is turned to the left. Both are face to face for the first time. They clasp hands together at mid-height, torsos leaning toward one another.

you will with all the saints have strength to grasp. With hands still clasped, the father helps the child rise to his feet, and both stand, facing one another.

the breadth and the length. Both father and child take a step backward, away from one another, hands separating with a small impulse; the arms extend sideways at shoulder height, the palms of one facing the palms of the other. The movement is done with a "breath" impulse and the extended arms should have a feeling of length and openness, without tension.

the height and the depth. The father and the child both raise arms overhead in a gesture of praise and thanksgiving. (The father's hands are not directing the child's by touch. At this point, the child is *mirroring* the father's gestures.) Then both bow, lowering arms, right knees touching the floor. (These movements are a *response* to God, rather than a picturing of height or depth.)

until, knowing the love of Christ, which is beyond all knowl-

edge. The father leans to the child and places his hands on, or slightly above, the child's head, *blessing* as he does so.

you are filled with the utter fullness of God. The father lowers his hands to the child's shoulders and imperceptibly lifts him to a standing position. His hands then continue in a downward, blessing motion. He remains in a reverent kneeling position as the child stands, face lifted, arms simply to the sides. They remain motionless, resting in this blessing.

Glory be to him whose power, working in us, can do infinitely more than we can ask or imagine; glory be to him from generation to generation in the church and in Christ Jesus for ever and ever. Amen. Father and child raise arms in praise. The father rises to his feet and both circle around, joyously.

Circle Dances

Dance is as old as the human race. When we read about the religions of the earliest people we find that all the important aspects of life were danced and brought into relation with God. In the ancient times there were three main forms of dance: *the circle dance* (circling around a place or object set it apart as holy—remember the line of the psalm, "I wash my hands in innocence, and go about thy altar, O Lord") *the procession;* and *dances of ecstasy.* (See Oesterley, *Sacred Dance: A Study in Comparative Folklore,* New York: Macmillan, 1923.)

King David's famous dance while bringing the ark of God to his city must have been a processional dance winding through the countryside, as well as a personal dance of ecstasy, as he leapt and whirled, praising God with abandon (2 Samuel 6).

In the early church the concept of the "ring dance of the angels" was that when the redeemed on earth danced, the angels in an invisible but real way joined them in the dance. People were exorted to dance, but to dance in the fear of the Lord, as St. Ambrose put it. (For a complete history of the church fathers' writings on dance, and dance through the Middle Ages in the church, read E.L. Backman's fascinating account in *Religious Dances in the Christian Church and in Popular Medicine,* London: Allen & Unwin, 1952.)

The circle dances described below have been tried with congregations many times and have met with great approval. They have been used as conclusions to eucharistic liturgies (after the final blessing), and as part of noneucharistic liturgies of all varieties.

"How Good and Pleasant It Is"

So many people have prayed, "Lord that we may be one!" Sometimes a group of worshipers experience the Spirit's descending and wafting through them, weaving his way between one and another. At these times we have an intimation of the glowing warmth of unity. Here is a quiet group dance of thanksgiving for such times using a setting of Psalm 133 composed by Nick Hodsdon.

How good and pleasant it is / For brothers to dwell together, / How good and pleasant it is, / How good and pleasant it is. Form two concentric circles with the same number of people in each. All will walk slowly around in their circle, the inside circle to the right (or counterclockwise), the outside circle to the left. While walking, everyone extends the right hand out to the side to touch the right hands of the people in the other circle as they pass in the opposite direction. The whole first verse is taken up with this meditative walking and hand "brushing" movement. Look at one another as you touch and pass.

Like the dew of Mt. Hermon that falls, / The dew of Mt. Hermon that falls . . . The two circles stop moving and everyone faces someone in the other circle. (Decide beforehand in the practice session what the exact cue for stopping will be. I sometimes stand in the center of both circles to help guide together those who need partners.) Everyone in the inside circle slowly lifts the right hand, from below, forward and upward to about chest height, palm facing up, as the people in the outside circle raise their right hands backwards and overhead, and slowly lower them (as gently as dew), palms facing downward, till they meet their partner's right hand on the second word, "falls." (This will feel like movement in suspended time.)

Upon Mt. Zion's height, / Upon Mt. Zion's height! Holding the right hands together, repeat the above directions with the left hand, only in reverse: those on the inside circle raise their left hands backward and overhead and then lower them while the people on the outside circle slowly extend their left hands forward and upward to meet the joined right hands, while their partners' left hands descend (to make what Nick calls a hand sandwich). As this second verse ends, everyone's hands are joined together with their partner's, held about chest height in a loving clasp.

For the Lord commanded there / The blessing, Life, forever . . . All in the inside circle will "bless" their partners by placing the hands on the partner's head and slowly passing them over the shoulders downward, until they fall back to the blesser's sides. This flowing touch could evoke the feeling of the only line of the psalm which was not included in the song: "It is like the precious oil upon the head, running down upon the beard, upon the beard of Aaron, running down on the collar of his robes!"

The Lord commanded there, / Of Life, forever more! All in the outside circle now bless their partners in the same way as they were blessed. Repeat the entire dance as many times as you want, each time with a different partner.

HOW GOOD AND PLEASANT IT IS

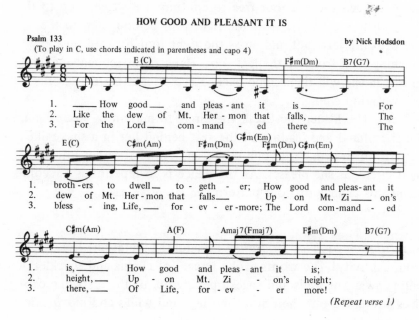

Psalm 133

by Nick Hodsdon

(To play in C, use chords indicated in parentheses and capo 4)

1. ___ How good ___ and pleas-ant it is ___ For
2. Like the dew of Mt. Her-mon that falls, ___ The
3. For the Lord ___ com-mand - ed there ___ The

1. broth-ers to dwell ___ to - geth - er; How good and pleas-ant it
2. dew of Mt. Her-mon that falls ___ Up - on Mt. Zi ___ on's
3. bless - ing, Life, ___ for - ev - er-more; The Lord com-mand - ed

1. is, ___ How good and pleas - ant it is;
2. height, ___ Up - on Mt. Zi - on's height;
3. there, ___ Of Life, for - ev - er more!

(Repeat verse 1)

"Hineh Ma Tov" is a dance of Jewish origin. The words, also from Psalm 133, are "Behold, how good and pleasant it is when brothers dwell in unity!" I have been taught several versions of this dance, and offer this simple one. I do not know if it is completely authentic, but people love to dance it.

Hineh Ma Tov (Psalm 133)

Opening formation: a circle, facing counterclockwise. Everyone's left hand is placed over his or her own left shoulder. The right hand holds onto the left hand of the person in front. Bodies are consciously held upright, with long straight backs.

There are two steps which I will call chorus and variation. Practice them first and then put on the music. ("Hineh Ma Tov" is recorded on many Jewish folk albums.)

Chorus: Take four steps forward (counterclockwise) beginning with the right foot. Bend the knee after each step (i.e., right forward and bend right knee, left forward, and bend left knee, etc.). Then take eight running steps (double time) in the same direction. Repeat the sequence of four slow steps followed by eight running steps. Face center.

Variation: Holding hands shoulder height, step to the right with the right foot, cross left foot behind, step to the right with the right foot and cross left foot forward. (Just touch it in front without putting weight on it, as the sequence reverses to the left and you need the left foot free to continue.) Reverse: step to the left with the left foot, cross the right foot behind, step to the left with the left foot and cross the right foot forward, just touching it in front of the left foot. Repeat this sequence. (The chorus music will then come back. Keep alternating the chorus and variation steps.)

Note: The leader can break the circle formation by disengaging the right hand and leading all the rest behind her in a snake-like pattern, or drawing everyone closer and closer together into a tight circle, as she pleases. As the dance is so repetitious I recommend this change of floor pattern for interest's sake.

Miriam

(Contributed by Nick Hodsdon) Freedom! Liberation! Release from captivity! The words evoke images of chains and shackles falling away, of walls and cages opening up, of the erstwhile captives stretching out their arms and legs and wings and *moving,* in unfettered joy.

Fetters and bondage may be physical or they may be political or they may be psychological, but, in all cases, that which shackles is that which hinders movement. So free-flowing movement is a universal image for freedom and release from that which restricts people and holds them back from their potential.

Conversely, with most of us it can be the moving that brings the freedom. The very act of stretching after a nap, of reaching out to another during the greeting of peace, liberates us and initiates the good feeling of physical freedom, and I think that in turn helps us to grow freer both spiritually and emotionally. And the rejoicing in unfettered freedom finds its fullest, most beautiful vision in the dance.

The Hebrew Bible is a testament of God's saving activity for his people. The keystone of that activity is his liberating them from bondage in Egypt, and the most dramatic moment of this story is the Hebrews' dance of escape across the miraculously parted sea. The various writers refer to this event again and again during the thousand years of the Old Testament's formation, and some scholars say that the very earliest words of the whole Bible may well be those of Moses' and Aaron's sister, Miriam, immediately after this dash to safety: "Then Miriam, the prophetess, the sister of Aaron, took a timbrel in her hand; and all the women went out after her with timbrels and dancing. And Miriam sang to them: 'Sing to the Lord, for he has triumphed gloriously; the horse and his rider he has thrown into the sea.'" (Exodus 15:20-21)

To experience the feeling that the chanting and dancing must have given the newly liberated Hebrews, some groups might wish to try putting themselves in Miriam's place, when the wonder and thankfulness and praise overflowed in dance among these celebrators. With a tambourine, "Miriam" (the leader, moving with a sliding step) leads them in a circle, clapping and chanting "SING to the LORD! (clap-clap)/GLOry and POWer! (clap-clap)/ The HORSE and the RIDer, (clap-clap)/ Thrown INto the SEA!" (clap-clap). (Repeat five or six times, letting the growing chant and the praise move people into any natural expressions of physical freedom.)

Carla De Sola and I tried this once at a workshop on liberation during a summer convention of the Christian Life Communities. The participants, all "nondancers," found themselves lifting their heads, clapping high and low, spinning around in the clapping, sweeping out their arms in a gesture of release; through God's power, throwing the strictures into the sea. Praising God the Liberator in this way proved to be exhilarating and deeply prayerful.

"The Spirit is a-Movin'"

(Contributed by Nick Hodsdon) Another dance celebrating the freedom given by the Holy Spirit is based on an old folk song from the Southern black tradition—another tradition of long-sought and hard-won liberation. We frequently end prayer gatherings and liturgies with this as a closing hymn. Of the many contemporary versions of this old song, this is the one we like best:

Well, well, well, who's that a-calling? Participants walk among each other, stepping on the right foot, then bending the right knee slightly; then the left foot, left knee, etc., clapping hard on every other beat.

Well, well, well, take your neighbor's hand. Take anyone's
hand.

*Well, well, well, daylight's a-dawning, 'cause the Spirit is
a-movin', all over this land.* Circle in twos.

The Spirit is a-movin' to set people free! Drop hands. Hold
wrists together as if shackled; bow over chained hands as if captive. Gradually let the Spirit raise the hands up, which causes the
back to straighten, the head to lift. On the word *free,* the chains
break and the hands can fly up and apart in release.

The Spirit is a-callin' us all to liberty. Turn in place, arms up,
rejoicing in the freedom.

Brothers and sisters, side by side. All gather together in a tight
group, slightly bent over.

All standin' up and they won't hide! The group bursts apart,
all standing up straight and free, arms sweeping up and out in
liberty. Then repeat from *"Well, well, well."*

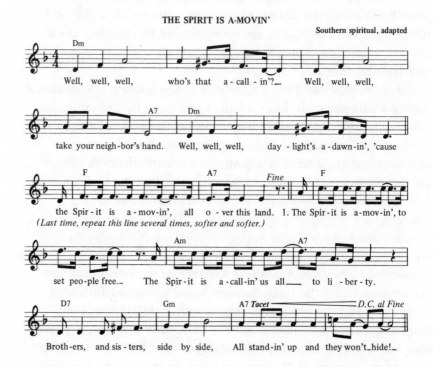

THE SPIRIT IS A-MOVIN'

Southern spiritual, adapted

118

This dance-prayer for peace could be used after liturgies, or during retreats when a break is needed. It becomes livelier and livelier.

Formation: A circle, all facing center, sitting on the floor on their heels.

And everyone 'neath their vine and fig tree shall live in peace and un-a-fraid. The leader extends the right hand to the right side and looks to the right. As soon as this is done the person on the leader's right extends the right hand in the same way and so on, until the entire circle has right hands extended to the sides. Everyone in the circle is responsible for pacing this sequence so that the last person extends his or her hand on "unafraid."

And everyone 'neath their vine and fig tree shall live in peace and un-a-fraid. The sequence is reversed. The leader extends the left hand to the left (keeping the right hand where it is), and takes hold of the right hand of the person on the left. Then the person on the leader's left extends the left hand and takes hold of the right hand of the next person, and so on, until by the end of the verse all hands are joined.

And into plowshares turn their swords. All rise to their knees and, extending their right legs, lunge forward, with joined hands converging toward the center.

Nations shall learn war no more. All lean backward, extending arms upward and open.

And into plowshares turn their swords. Repeat as before.

Nations shall learn war no more. Come to standing, again raising arms with a feeling of openness. Drop hands in order to begin again.

Repeat the entire song and the complete sequence, but this time standing. When this is done, either end the dance or keep repeating the song with the mood becoming increasingly exuberant, moving as described below:

The dance now changes. The leader links right arms with the person on the right and they swing together, skipping all around in a complete circle. The leader then extends the left hand to the next person (second person from the right) and swings in the same way while the person he or she just swung swings the person to the leader's left. This keeps going till 2-6-6-8 people are all swinging, moving as in the square dance "grand right and left" pattern, but making complete circles. When the leader and his or her first partner meet again (usually at the other side of the circle) they form a bridge and everyone goes under, each couple making a bridge themselves as soon as they emerge from under the arms of the couple in front of them.

This is very informal by now. Everyone should be clapping and skipping around with partners, improvising in whatever way they like.

VINE AND FIG TREE

Text from Micah 4:3b-4   by Shalom Altman

And eve - ry one 'neath their vine and fig tree shall live in

peace and un - a - fraid; And eve - ry fraid; And in - to plow-shares

turn their swords; na - tions shall learn war no more.

"A Gift to be Simple"

If one thinks of religious dance in America the Shakers always come to mind, for they were a religious sect for whom dance was an integral aspect of their worship. Founded in England, they came to the East and Midwest in the late eighteenth century and created many songs and dances to express their delight in God. (For further reading about their colorful and moving history see Edward Andrews, *The Gift to be Simple: Songs, Dances and Rituals of the American Shakers*, Dover Publications, 1962.)

"A Gift to be Simple" is one of the best known examples of their dances and songs. It is the original melody from which the popular church song "Lord of the Dance" is derived. The dance was taught to me by a Quaker who was living in the vicinity of a Shaker village. I was led to understand that this was an authentic version.

Opening formation: a circle, all facing center.

'Tis the gift to be simple, 'tis the gift to be free. All take four steps toward the center, beginning with the right foot (r,l,r,l). Hands are held in front of the body, about waist height, palms facing upward. Initiated by a gentle wrist movement, the hands pulse upward and downward. (This up-and-down movement with upturned hands was thought of as a gesture to receive grace.)

120

'Tis the gift to come down where we ought to be. All take four steps back to place (r,l,r,l). The palms face downward as you walk backward, and shake in a small down-and-up direction. (This movement, with turned down palms, was used to signify shaking out bad influences, or "all that is carnal." There is a Shaker song with the words, "Come life, Shaker life, come life eternal, shake, shake out of me all that is carnal.")

And when we find ourselves in the place just right, we will be in the valley of love and delight. Repeat the above pattern: four steps into the center and four steps back to place.

When true simplicity is gained. Bring hands to prayer position (palms together, fingertips pointing upward). Step to the right with the right foot and bring the left foot to meet the right, bending both knees. Reverse to the left on the words, "simplicity is gained."

To bow and to bend we shall not be ashamed. Repeat the above pattern (stepping and bending to the right and then to the left).

To turn, turn will be our delight. Keeping hands in the same prayer position, turn in place by making a small circle to the right (step r,l,r,l). End facing the center.

Till by turning, turning we come round right. Reverse. (Make a small circle to the left, stepping l,r,l,r).

Note: The quality of the dance is one of simplicity, joy, gentleness. Listen to Judy Collins's arrangement called "Simple Gifts" on Electra Records, *Judy Collins,* for a fine rendition.

"We See the Lord"

Another simple dance, especially fitting as a response to the text of Revelation 7, is set to "We See the Lord." This song is often sung at prayer meetings and appears on the record *Hymn of the Universe,* put out by the Word of God Community in Ann Arbor, Michigan. It was written by James Byrne and is reprinted here with his permission.

> We see the Lord! (2x)
> And He is high and
> lifted up, and His
> train fills the temple. (2x)
> The angels cry holy (3x)
> Is the Lord!

We see the Lord! (2x)
And His face shines
forth as a light in
the temple. (2x)
The seraphs cry holy (3x)
Is the Lord!

We hear the Lord ! (2x)
And His word issues
forth and resounds
through the temple. (2x)
The elders cry Amen (3x)
It is so!

We bless the Lord! (2x)
And as incense goes
up, so our prayers
fill the temple. (2x)
The people cry glory (3x)
To the Lord!

I have designed a very simple dance which can be done by
almost everyone with one practice session. All form a circle. If
the circle gets too large, form concentric circles (one inside the
other). The circles will move in opposite directions—one clockwise,
one counterclockwise, and so on. All walk around in the circle,
arms held forward, hands at about shoulder level, palms facing
upward. (This is done with a feeling of offering oneself and praising God.) Think of *leading with your heart* as you walk, not
holding back in self-consciousness but keeping your weight forward, really offering yourself. If flowers are available (the text
in Revelation mentions palms) they can be held by each person,
taking the place of the hand gesture.

Walking is interrupted without stopping the flow by bowing
as the last two lines of each stanza are sung, as follows: On "the
angels cry holy" all stop and bow, keeping the weight either on
the right or left foot, whichever is forward, bending the knees and
curving the torso forward while lowering the arms to the sides in
a gentle downward swinging motion. On the repeat of "the angels
cry holy" all straighten up, swinging arms upward, torso and head

lifting up high. On the third repeat all swing down into the bow and on "Is the Lord!" all straighten up, bringing hands back to the middle position (held out in front of the body), ready to begin again. This down-up-down swinging-bowing movement is done in a soft, sustained manner, conducive to really praying the lines.

Each stanza is performed in the same manner (walking and bowing) but people may want to improvise different gestures in response to the words "His face shines forth," or "His word issues forth," or "as incense goes up."

Special Occasions

"In those days Mary arose and went with haste into the hill country, to a city of Judah, and she entered the house of Zechariah and greeted Elizabeth. And when Elizabeth heard the greeting of Mary, the babe leaped in her womb." (Luke 1:39-41)

That leap in the womb, in the heart, among friends, suggests that a baby's baptism might be celebrated by a dance—that a poetic leap at the approach of Jesus might be actualized!

Here is one dance suggestion with natural gestures and movements expressing the deep sense of quiet joy on such an occasion, set to the gentle song of Sister Germaine, "All of My Life" (*Hymnal for Young Christians,* F.E.L. Publications, Ltd.).

The refrain is sung twice while the parents with the baby, the godparents and immediate community process up the aisle. They stop in front, in the center, all the friends encircling the baby and parents. On "For creation, praise," the baby is lifted up high for all to see. On "For salvation, praise," the group around the baby gently lay hands on the baby, as a blessing. On "For all mankind, praise," all slowly turn around, widening the circle as they do so, arms extended to bless and welcome all in the church.

As the refrain is sung, the center group joins hands and circles around the baby and parents, while all in the pews raise their arms, reaching up and then forward, extended toward the baby. This should be done slowly, with a sense of speaking to God and praising the child. The arms are lowered as the refrain ends.

The congregation may need someone to lead them in this, since the center group is doing something different from them, and the tendency would be to watch and not move themselves. However, the center group could also just raise their arms if this seems simpler, instead of circling around the child.

Verse 2 could be danced by a solo dancer, or just sung; the gestures for the refrain would be the same as before. On verse 3, the center group bows deeply, slowly and profoundly, head and chest lowering, arms at the sides. For the final refrain, the center group joins hands around the baby, and the congregation joins hands with one another, and all raise their arms high in a final gesture of praise, with head and chest lifted up.

In praise of water

Primary school children at the Convent of the Sacred Heart in New York City, under the direction of Dorita Beh, danced to the following verses for a liturgy on water:

"And the Spirit of God was moving over the face of the waters." (Genesis 1:1).

"He leads me beside still waters, he restores my soul" (Psalm 23:3).

"His going forth is sure as the dawn; he will come to us as the showers, as the spring rains that water the earth" (Hosea 6:3).

"As a hart longs for flowing streams, so longs my soul for thee, O God" (Psalm 42:1).

"Waters shall break forth in the wilderness, and streams in the desert; the burning sand shall become a pool, and the thirsty ground springs of water" (Isaiah 35:6-7).

"Whoever drinks of the water that I shall give him will never thirst; the water that I shall give him will become in him a spring of water welling up to eternal life" (John 4:14).

The music used was Maurice Ravel's Introduction and Allegro for harp, string quartet, flute and clarinet. These, and others, could also be used for a baptism liturgy, the children in the community preparing beforehand their own dances to the verses. What is needed for preparation is someone who can speak to the children about the meaning of water in baptism, about water as a sign of life, and who can draw out of the children ways to move that express the images and moods and feelings of the lines—for example, the yearning (stretching movement) in Psalm 42, or the new life and refreshment (open, bursting, bubbly movement) of Isaiah 35.

A joyful children's dance with candles

This dance should combine a sense of reverence with spontaneous joy. Prepare the children ahead of time by discussing with them the beauty of the candle and how they have to hold it so it will not blow out—and how its flickering is like the bouncy spirit of the children themselves, but its innermost point is still yet vibrant, like each one's spirit, warm and filled with unique energy.

> The little light of mine, O Lord,
> I'm going to let it shine,
> This little light of mine, O Lord,
> I'm going to let it shine,
> This little light of mine, O Lord,
> I'm going to let it shine,
> Let it shine, let it shine, let it shine.

Children enter from all over the church, walking joyfully, each holding a candle. They converge in front of the altar. All the people in the pews sing and clap.

> All over God's kingdom, I'm going to let it shine,
> All over God's kingdom, I'm going to let it shine,
> All over God's kingdom, I'm going to let it shine,
> Let it shine, let it shine, let it shine.

Prepare two leaders beforehand. One leads half the children around the altar to the right, and the other to the left, so that there are two circles moving around the altar, each in a different direction. On the last line, all stop and face the altar, raising their candles high.

> This little light of mine, O Lord,
> I'm going to let it shine,
> This little light of mine, O Lord,
> I'm going to let it shine,
> This little light of mine, O Lord,
> I'm going to let it shine,
> Let it shine, let it shine, let it shine.

All carefully place candles on the altar. As the children come, to the center of the altar, before going back down the aisle, tell them to let their inner light shine in any way each one wants, expressing it through movement, with a leap, a turn, a skip, etc. (Adults keep singing and clapping all the way through.)

Autumn

"The Winds of Autumn," words and music by Nick Hodsdon of the Omega Community in New York City, is a lovely, lilting piece that calls for a more trained dance group to choreograph it. The music is given below.

Here are some general suggestions: first, find someone to play the music while everyone in the group listens, eyes closed. The next step would be to improvise with the music. Perhaps half the group could be the wind, "blowing" through the church, and half "leaves," starting maybe in a pile on the floor, being tossed and turned as the wind blows, or being tossed out of their seats and blown to the front.

The second verse calls for more fast movement of hand-like leaf-rustling movements, and changing shapes, directions, relationships with one another.

The third verse lends itself to circling the altar with the grapevine, or other hearty folk-like steps, celebrating the harvest in a banquet-like way, perhaps with gestures of toasts or passing the cup.

The last verse suggests the more serious prayer of the group. Slow down the tempo of the movements. Use unison movements of reaching in prayer, washing or purging, turning and facing front with a new sense of openness, and finally movements of embracing, or sharing of oneself with others.

THE WINDS OF AUTUMN

words and music by Nick Hodsdon

1. The winds of Au- - tumn blow   The winds of clear__ Sep-
2. The leaves are chang - ing fast   The leaves of pure__ Oc -
3. The cheer of har - vest glows   The cheer of bright__ No -
4. O   God, blow through our lives,   And wash us with__ your

1. tem - ber   Stream-ing in__ the wind   And whisk - ing out__ the
2. to - ber   Turn - ing in__ the wind   The col - ors flash__ and
3. vem - ber   Cir - cles in__ the wind   And rip - ens in__ the
4. wind song,   Turn us as__ the leaves,   Make all our col - ors

1. rain - bows   We feel the wind   clean and as-trin-gent   winds of Au - tumn
2. trem - ble   We're turn-ing too,   we're grow-ing New as   leaves are chang - ing
3. laugh - ter   We rip - en too,   our fruit ac-crue as   Cheer of har - vest
4. glow - ing,   Bring us to bear,   free us to share The   har - vest of__ our

1. blow.
2. fast.   *(Guitar)*
3. glows.
4. lives.

©1970 Nick Hodsdon

Here are two dance suggestions for congregational use to express for the Lord's goodness. The first is suitable for any time; the second is designed more specifically for the season of harvest and fullness.

The first is a litany of thanksgiving:

> For your faithful love, we thank you, Lord.
> For the flowing life of the Spirit, we thank you, Lord.
> For the presence of your Son among us, we thank you, Lord.
> For the dying, changing leaves, we thank you, Lord.
> For the fullness of harvest, we thank you, Lord.
>   (and on and on and on . . .)

Ask everyone in the congregation to stand and to think of something that means a lot. Then ask for a group of volunteers (around ten) to step forward and form a semicircle facing the others, and ask each to think of a simple movement to express this thankful thought. The person at one end of the semicircle begins by *speaking* out loud and *moving* to the spoken word of thanksgiving, and then *repeating* it, with the gestures, while all the others up front and in the pews do the words and movements.

For example, one person said, "For the fullness of life, we thank you, Lord," and simply jumped up and threw his arms in the air, and all up front and in the pews did the same after him. (It's amazing to find out how much people can do in the pews.

129

They can turn, bend, jump, etc.)

Continue in this manner till all in the semicircle have had a turn. Some general ending is called for to tie it all together. One suggestion is to have the organist or guitarist play a strong folk melody, like "The King of Glory" which has a *hora* beat, and have all in the pews clap to the rhythm while the people in front dance. They can join hands and circle around, improvising a small folk dance on the spot, using the grapevine step, the *hora* step, or just simply circle around, running, skipping, turning, and coming all together into the center with upraised arms for an ending.

This litany can take on a joyful air or a solemn one. In the latter case, close with a prayer like "Let all that is within me thank the Lord," with everyone bowing deeply.

"All Good Gifts"

The second thanksgiving dance is to "All Good Gifts" from *Godspell.* Fill a large basket to overflowing with vines, spices, apples, oranges, flowers, etc. On the first verse the leader, who carries the basket, and as many people as want to (adults and children) slowly process down the aisles. All who are in the procession walk behind the leader in a double line, and sing and sway their arms in any pattern that seems natural. As the first verse ends the leader will stop in front of the main altar and those in line will move to the side and in front of the leader, as in an informal gathering.

On the first line of the chorus (*"All good gifts around us"*), everyone makes a complete circle, arms outstretched as if to say that each person in the church and in the world is a gift. On *"Are sent from heaven above,"* all slowly lift up their arms and heads in praise to the Father. On *"Then thank the Lord, O, thank the Lord,"* all deeply and slowly bow. On *"For all his love,"* all rise and each embraces the nearest person. (If space permits, ask those in the pews to also dance this chorus.)

If you're using the record, or have musicians who can play the musical interlude before the second verse, have each person up by the altar take out one of the items in the basket and walk and dance with it down a side aisle, moving with gentle, simple swaying motions, filling the church with the beauty of the gifts. All return back via the center aisle by the end of the last verse, and place their gifts around the altar. The leader's basket should still be filled with leaves and flowers even after everyone has taken something from it. He or she can dance with it as the rest are moving down the aisles, or just stand there with it upraised, facing the people. On the final chorus the same movements are repeated as before. All then return to their seats, leaving their gifts and the basket by the altar. If this is done before the presentation of the gifts, the regular procession with the gifts of bread and wine could now begin, and the chorus be repeated.

During the Thanksgiving season (or any other time of the year) why not dance or use gestures with grace at the main meal? The very word "grace" implies the idea of a receiving and a "graceful" response. Simple gestures can give new meaning to the many similar words we use with which to thank God. Gestures with arms upraised (toward God), toward the food, toward one another, and a reverential bow would be appropriate for any number of graces. For example:

A table blessing

Praise God from whom all blessings flow. All extend hands toward the table (or altar).

Praise him all creatures here below. All join hands around the table.

Praise him above, ye heavenly host. All raise hands high, heads lifted.

Praise Father, Son, and Holy Ghost. All lower arms, hands still joined, and bow.

Pause in silence.

For the season of all saints and thanksgiving I'd like to suggest a circle dance set to "The Canticle of Brother Sun," which can be found on the record *Sons of the Morning* by Leo Nestor, put out by World Library Publications. St. Francis certainly knew how to praise his Lord and offer thanks. The dance, though it is simple, needs to be practiced ahead of time.

"The Canticle of Brother Sun"

Opening position: a chain, arms held around each other's shoulders, at the back of the church.

All slowly move down the aisle in chain formation as the music starts. The knees bend after each step (step, bend; step, bend; etc.). End in a circle around the altar. The melody of the first chorus will begin, but there are no words as yet. All do the chorus step, circling the altar in a clockwise direction, hands joined. The dance is done the same way each time the chorus is repeated, whether sung or instrumental. Chorus:

> Alleluia, alleluia, strike the harp and sing,
> Alleluia, alleluia, I will wake the dawn,
> For it is given to man to praise his Lord
> As long as he shall breathe.

Chorus sequence: Moving clockwise, all start with the right foot and step r,l,r; l,r,l. (alleluia), r,l,r; l,r,l. (alleluia). (In each set of three little steps the first foot advances forward along the circle, the second catches up to it, closing behind it, and the third step advances again.) On "strike the harp and sing" all do the grapevine step (cross the right foot in front, step left with the left foot, cross the right foot in back and step left with the left foot again). Do eight steps in all, the whole pattern repeats on the second line. On the third line, "For it is given to man to praise his Lord," all swoop toward the center, raising arms upward, and then swoop backwards, arms lowering. On the last line all swoop again toward the center and at the peak of the movement let go of hands and make a complete turn in place to the right, arms still raised, and then move backward to the original circle.

Verse: Each verse is different and is usually improvised by all in a free manner, but it can be choreographed if the dance is to be presented. Movements will vary naturally according to whatever is being praised. St. Francis praises Brother Sun in the first verse (use open, full movements of receiving light, warmth), Sister Moon in the second (find movements that catch the mystery of the moon, its rising, its beauty), Brother Wind and Sister Water in the third verse: try different wind qualities (soft, sweeping), and then quiet water movements (rippling, drinking, bathing). On the third verse ("And now be praised and blessed my Lord in this fair canticle, and I will sing and serve my Lord, with great humility"), all slowly move toward the center, arms being gradually lifted, and then deeply bow and lower to the floor until the entire torso is bent over, head on the floor, body resting on knees and heels. The right arm ends forward, palm facing upward on the floor, and the left arm is backward alongside the body, palm facing downward. Hold.

"I will rejoice in Jerusalem, and be glad in my people; no more shall be heard in it the sound of weeping and the cry of distress. No more shall there be in it an infant that lives but a few days, or an old man who does not fill out his days, for the child shall die a hundred years old" (Isaiah 56:19-20).

I want to encourage those who work on liturgies and especially on liturgical dances to think of the elderly and include them specifically in the services, bringing to their attention and the attention of the congregation the gifts and services older people have to offer. (Recall Peter's mother-in-law jumping up to serve everybody after being touched by the Lord, her body and spirit united.) I want to share with you an experience of the "young-at-heart" dancing—a small but important experience that furthers my belief that somehow through movement, no matter at what age, a person's spiritual energy (usually waiting, in a dormant state, to be called on) is released. Not only does it become a joyful and deeply meaningful experience for those directly involved, but everyone benefits from the real outpouring of gentle love and reverence that finds expression.

You may wonder if older people will be at all receptive to the idea of dancing. Certainly not everybody will be called in this direction, and many will be cautious because of physical weaknesses. But if even a few respond much will be gained. For the person initiating the idea in a parish, it is important to remember that all is possible where there is trust, an invocation of the Spirit, and belief in the outcome. By this I mean that the priest or sister or lay person suggesting the dance should know the older people, or be introduced by someone who has established a relationship of trust with them, and should have the hope that with the Holy Spirit's help the joy and life in each person will emerge, and, finding expression, grow into a fountain of praise!

Who knows what can happen! I want to share with you a scene that took place in a liturgy at a charismatic conference in California—a brief aside from the elderly. The mass was the conclusion of a workshop on dance, music, art and prayer, and was held in a large, cleared area. Two people came in wheelchairs, unable to walk, and only with great difficulty could they coordinate their arm gestures with what little speech they were able to manage. They had wanted to go to a healing workshop held at the same time but it was filled. After the final blessing there was a circle dance and then spontaneous joyous dancing broke out. Suddenly someone rolled to the center of the circle one of the disabled persons in his wheelchair. Another person grabbed the wheelchair of the other person and they began a dance, moving them around in a large figure eight pattern, with everyone else clapping, laughing and dancing around them. It was a high moment of resurrection! The man and woman were laughing in their wheelchairs, waving their arms, utterly gleeful, so glad to be included in the celebration. They later said they were so happy they came to this workshop, that they felt much, much better and hadn't had such fun in years! No one there will ever forget it.

Back to the elderly. I still feel blessed by a recent meeting I had with a small group of women I met from the Golden Age Club of St. Nicholas of Tolentine, in Jamaica, N.Y., under the direction of Anthony Fasano. They were beautifully receptive to the dance suggestion I will outline below, as well as to the Our Father done in gestures, and are looking forward to doing both in a liturgy. When the mini-workshop began and I mentioned that dance and liturgy was my special interest they seemed rather confused ("What! Dancing on the altar next!"), but by the end of forty-five minutes of easy limbering exercises and slow and fast simple patterns and then the dance-prayers it seemed the most natural idea in the world to them. And as I tried to convey earlier, when they danced I felt a release of grace and beauty from them, and was surrounded by love. I received as they flowed. (It occurs to me that the release of the gifts of the elderly is connected to their letting go of any natural power or status that they might have become entrenched in or have identified themselves with. The people I met were really "poor in spirit.")

I would therefore like to see a recognition and stimulation of the wisdom, love and other gifts the elderly have and could share with a community. This concept could be brought out through this simple blessing dance, set to Nick Hodsdon's beautiful song "The Golden Years," written specially for the elderly. (A poem with words like the ending of his song could be substituted, with harmonious music played in the background.) After communion, and after a few moments of silence, the song would begin and all would simply listen to it. Near the end of the song four older people, representative of all the elderly in the congregation, would walk down the aisle, and, reaching the sanctuary, in front of the altar, bless four younger people who would be standing there, waiting for them (or they could have slowly walked there from different points in the church, arriving at the same time). The blessing is conveyed through the gestures, the younger ones copying the older ones, as in a "mirror" game. This should be rehearsed previously. (Older people dancing with younger ones would help people be aware of the beauty of a lovimg communion among diverse ages, as well as emphasizing the special gifts that age brings. However, as in the Golden Age Club, it was also beautiful to see the elderly just dancing with one another in this way.)

Here are the gestures coordinated with the song:

The four older people would begin slowly walking toward the altar after the first or second stanza is completed, depending on the size of the church. They stop when they are about three feet apart from, and face to face with, one of the four younger persons. (Adapt this distance so that the gestures can be done comfortably.) On *"And when does the store house have the most to share,"* the four couples are still facing one another, preparing to move, looking in each other's eyes. (One could think, "Father/Mother, give me a blessing . . . ")

On *of memories,* without a break in the slow flowing movement just described, each person will extend the right hand forward and gesture toward the partner's heart.

On *And thoughts to share* each person will clasp both hands of the partner, at about chest level.

On *and time to spare* all will simply hold still in the above position, looking at one another.

On *You don't throw away gold* each set will embrace and then slowly walk off together.

All these gestures should be performed with dignity and love, gentleness and ease. As the song began in silence, let there be a few moments of stillness before the final prayers.

I have loved you with an everlasting love; therefore I have continued my faithfulness to you. Again I will build you, and you shall be built, O virgin Israel! Again you shall adorn yourself with timbrels, and shall go forth in the dance of the merrymakers. (Jeremiah 31:3-4)

Take my yoke upon you, and learn from me; for I am gentle and lowly in heart. (Matthew 11:29)

It's not quite "merrymaking" yet, but a start. Let the congregation take up their timbrels, and let's see who will join in.

GOLDEN YEARS

Commissioned by
Presbyterian Senior Services

by Nick Hodsdon

136

beau - ti - ful!_____ It's beau - ti - ful.

Who wants to live with - out fall?_____

3. There's gold and there's sil - ver in the au - tumn years._____

Well, when does the har - vest come 'round?_____

And when does the store-house have the most to share,_____

of mem - o - ries,_____

and wis - dom,_____ and

thoughts to share,_____ and

time to spare? You don't throw a - way gold._____

Every lifetime is punctuated by critical turning points which require the regathering of one's inner resources and the redefinition
of one's relationship to the community. The celebration described
here, while suitable for persons of any age, was based in its con-
ception on the idea that older people upon retirement have special

A ritual of retirement

137

gifts to give and a new role to play in the church and in the world, but they need to be affirmed by a praying community for these gifts to be called forth, and to attain a deeper understanding of the role of the Spirit in their lives. These gifts may be of all sorts, from the practical to the intangible. I have felt especially blessed by a few older people who, having dropped all worldly strivings and self-images, just quietly radiated an outgoing love and attention that warmed me from top to bottom.

The calling forth. a) The people who wish to be renewed and have prepared themselves for the ceremony come forward, each with one or two friends, and stand around the altar in a circle. Their friends form an outer circle around them.

b) A selection from scripture is read, possibly 1 Peter 2:4-9.

c) All sing "Priestly People" (Lucien Deiss, *Biblical Hymns and Psalms,* Volume I, World Library Publications). On the words "God's chosen people," in the antiphon, the outer circle of friends lay hands on the shoulders of those in the center. On "Sing praise to the Lord" all raise their arms overhead with a feeling of openness and trust in the Lord. (Suggested verses: 1, 2, 4, 6, 7 and 13.)

The renunciation (forgetting what lies behind). a) Philippians 3:7-14 is read.

b) Each person in the center (those being blessed), having written down beforehand whatever past negative feelings (such as despairs, disillusionments, feelings of failure, fears of the future, etc.) from which they wish to disengage, to "forget," either reads them aloud, or just takes the paper and silently casts it down in the center of the altar. A small fire could be prepared and the papers burned there by the presider, or they could be laid on a cross.

c) All sing "Don't Look Back." (It is hard to stand still while singing this song. The people could leisurely circle around the altar, with everyone clapping the rhythm, or walk around, as if on a journey, to various areas in the church, returning to the sanctuary.)

The affirmation (reaching out for that which lies ahead).
a) A selection is read, possibly Psalm 103:1-5, or Isaiah 40:28-31.

b) Each person reads a short credo of trust in God's plan and love for him/her, that each has prepared beforehand.

c) All around the altar (including the friends) sing "Spirit of the Living God" with the gestures (see below). (While this is happening the priest, at the altar, blesses them. He might simply stand, with arms upraised, and slowly turn in place, so as to include the entire inner circle of people.)

d) All in the congregation sing and move to "Spirit of the Living God," with the people at the altar leading them. The last line is changed, however, to "fall afresh on us." As this is sung, all will gently lower their arms around the shoulders of the persons on either side of them.

e) . . . silence . . . kiss of peace . . . rejoicing . . . food. (I would like to see the ritual included in the context of the eucharist, perhaps taking the place of the readings.)

DON'T LOOK BACK

Southern Baptist folk hymn   Adapted by Nick Hodsdon

1. Don't look back, good peo-ple, don't look back.
2. Greet each day, good peo-ple, greet each day.
3. Sing your song, good peo-ple, sing your song.
(Make up your own verses; any three words will do it!)

1   Don't look back, good peo-ple, don't look back.
2   Greet each day, good peo-ple, greet each day.
3   Sing your song, good peo-ple, sing your song.

Refrain
There's a race that we must run, and a vic-t'ry to be won. Ev-'ry hour gives us pow-er to go on.

The music for this song can be heard on the recording *Hymn of the Universe* (The Word of God Music, Ann Arbor, Michigan).

√ **"Spirit of the Living God"**

139

Spirit of the living God, fall afresh on me.
Spirit of the living God, fall afresh on me.
Melt me, mold me, fill me, use me.
Spirit of the living God, fall afresh on me.

Spirit of the living God. All stand up. Raise both arms up slowly in front of your body until they are held high overhead. (The movement comes alive when the head and chest lift along with the arms.)

fall afresh on me. Lower your arms, passing your palms a few inches in front of your face (which is still uplifted) and down the rest of your body until they rest by your sides. Feel as if your body is being bathed with freshness.

Spirit of the living God. Repeat the same movement as before.

fall afresh on me. Repeat as before.

Melt me, mold me. Slowly bow from the waist. Kneel (as if melting) if you are away from the pews.

fill me, use me. Slowly straighten up and lift your arms forward to about shoulder height, palms facing up. (Think of this gesture as an offering of yourself. Let your hands speak of you— of openness, readiness, of whatever feelings you have.)

Spirit of the living God. Repeat as before (lifting up your arms overhead).

fall afresh on me. Repeat as before.

Evening prayer

The following evening prayer was first choreographed for a group of five people on a special retreat. We became a family for that week, united by common experience in movement, prayer and song. The dance is set to Psalm 133 (134), and uses the music and text of Brother Norbert and the choir at St. Joseph's Abbey, Spencer, Massachusetts, available on BRC records.

Opening position: A circle formation. One or more candles are in the center and the rest of the lights are out. All are kneeling, sitting back on their heels, torsos bent forward, arms stretched out in front, palms facing upward, resting on the floor.

Note: The steps are done in unison, and performed in a slow, sustained manner. They are focused, and there is little extraneous movement.

140

Come, bless the Lord. Still resting on heels, all raise torso upright, hands coming to rest on knees, palms facing upward.

all you who serve the Lord. All bring hands in as if toward the heart and then extend them forward, slightly below shoulder height, with the feeling of serving. Palms are facing upward.

Who stand in the house of the Lord. All rise to knees, lowering arms to the sides. The chest lifts as the arms lower.

in the courts of the house of our God. Bring right leg forward and rise to feet as smoothly as possible. Arms are still at the sides.

Lift up your hands to the holy place. All slowly raise right hands straight upward, and at the same time bring left hands to about heart level, palm facing upward, fingers pointing sideways to the right, held about five inches from the torso. (The right hand travels further than the left hand, but both arrive in place at the same time.) Heads are lifted.

and bless the Lord through the night. All hold left hands in place while turning the torso to the right, placing the right hand, palm facing down, over the upturned left hand of the person to the right.

May the Lord bless you from Zion. Everyone takes one step backward and joins hands in the circle, fingertips pointing upward, palm to palm with the person on either side. Faces are lifted.

he who made both heaven and earth. All walk around in the circle, keeping the hand formation. The slow walking gives the sense of the endless circling of the planets.

Praise the Father, the Son and Holy Spirit, both now and forever, Amen. All face center and slowly cross hands over the breast, inclining the torso forward, as in a traditional bow.

Note: After a few minutes of silence people may want to sing or pray spontaneously.

The mystery of death

There are times when we are without words. Death is an occasion when people search for a way to give adequate expression to the intuitive, spiritual dimension. Throughout the ages at such times people have danced. Perhaps it is not an arbitrary juxtaposition of words: " . . . a time to mourn, and a time to dance." First we need to be in touch with our grief, and then we need to express our hope in order to be healed.

Dance is a link between the living and the dead. As I mentioned in the chapter on circle dances, the often referred to "ring-dance of the angels" concept of the early church depicted the blessed on earth dancing with the angels and blessed in heaven. The faithful on earth, while dancing the ring-dance, were joined in an invisible way by the angels in heaven. Basileios (344-407), Bishop of Caesarea, writes: "Could anything be more blessed than to imitate on earth the ring-dance of the angels and at dawn to raise our voices in prayer and by hymns and songs glorify the rising Creator." (See E. Louis Backman, *Religious Dances in the Christian Church and in Popular Medicine,* London: Allen & Unwin, 1952.)

St. Gregory of Nazianzus (ca. 369) writes that a dance is connected with a mystery, and by dancing one approaches God. In describing how martyrs should be honored, he says, "We must execute our triumphal ring-dance. Great throngs of people must perform a ring-dance for the martyrs in reverent honor of their precious blood." In a summary of dance in the church by the fourth century, Backman mentions watch-night services held in connection with festivals and martyrs and celebrated in church-yards or at gravesides. These dances were joyous. The faithful could only bring a triumphal dance as a gift to the martyr, and thus complete the work of the martyr. "Now it is for you yourselves to add what remains, so that you may offer a gift to the martyr himself." (Gregory of Nazianzus) These dances were also in expectation of blessings: healings, expulsions of devils, knowledge of things to come—all from the merits of the martyrs.

During the Middle Ages the dark and fearful side of death was ever present. The dead were feared: they might become demons and drag the living with them to the grave. The "danse macabre," or "dance of death," of the Middle Ages must have stemmed from the ravages of the plague and was probably a way of coping with the terror of the times. "Death," dressed in a skeleton costume (the original Halloween costume?) and dancing in grotesque ways, led people from all walks of life in a dance from life to death and beyond. No one was spared, neither pope nor lord nor common person.

People find a way to act out their fears and hopes. Margaret Fisk Taylor, in her book *A Time to Dance* (United Church Press, 1967), describes a fascinating example of the dance of death in connection with wakes for the dead in the fourteenth century. Guests were paired off, then sang and danced. When a sudden high note was sounded all stopped and became still. A mournful melody began and a young man would fall to the ground as if dead. The women then danced around him singing dirges. One by one they would bend over and kiss him, bringing him back to life. This ended with a general round dance. The sequence would then be repeated with a woman falling in the center as if dead, and the men kissing her back to life. This dance represents to me a charming, symbolic and intuitive way of coupling the resurrection with a life-giving act of love, and our breath with the Holy Spirit.

Oesterley, in *The Sacred Dance: A Study in Comparative Folklore* (Macmillan, 1923), describes dancing as part of the mourning and burial rites of the Jewish people. During the Talmudic period (around A.D. 500) the Ashkenazic and Sephardic Jews would keep up a monotonous and rhythmical stamping of feet while laudatory speeches were being said. Sephardic Jews would process around the corpse seven times concluding with "and continually may he walk in the land of life, and may his soul rest in the bond of life." (They perform this ritual to this day. I remember being led around and around my Sephardic grandfather's coffin when I was a young girl, though I had no idea of the significance.)

In our times we still see in New Orleans long lines of mourners singing and dancing behind the coffin bearers, accompanied by jazz musicians.

So we see that dance in relation to death is part of our religious history. What gestures and dances can we do today to help us meet our fears of death, and affirm our belief in the communion of saints both living and dead? I hope the following suggestions for congregations, dance groups and families will be helpful in this respect.

A meditation, based on Luke 20:27-40 ("He is not God of the dead, but of the living!"). First read the passage aloud. Then ask all, as part of their reflection on the reading, to sit very still, to be aware of the life within them, and to respond to the following suggestions:

Close your eyes. Sit comfortably erect, and quietly become aware of your breath and let your energy flow smoothly. Be

143

aware of your feet upon the floor, and the life in your legs, thighs, torso, arms, neck, head, bones and muscles. Observe the blood circulating. Be aware of your lungs contracting and expanding. Turn your palms upward. Feel the life, warmth and energy in the palms of your hands. Sense the life in the air both within and around you. Bend forward and touch your feet. Draw your arms upward alongside your body, raising your torso as you do so. Lift your arms upward in a gesture that will unite your body and heart to the Lord. Hold. Perceive your deep connection to the source of all love. (If you wish to, picture someone you know surrounded by God's light.) Slowly lower your hands, feeling them to be charged with loving energy. Open your eyes and turn to someone on either side of you, take that person's hands in your own and say, "He is God of the living." Give and receive this gesture with the person on the other side of you. Return your hands to your lap and be still for another minute, thanking God for his gift of life and asking for the gift of knowing that in God all that is will continue forever in a resurrected, new form.

"Amazing Grace." Another way of expressing our continuity of life in Christ might be a simple chain dance to the song "Amazing Grace." The dance leader, presider or deacon asks volunteers to join hands and follow him as he winds his way up and down the aisles, while the rest of the congregation sings. "Amazing Grace" lends itself to slow, prayerful walking steps. By the last verse all should be gathered around the altar. Adding an additional verse consisting of "alleluias" to the melody, all circle around the altar, arms upraised in praise and thanksgiving. One could imagine, as in the early "ring-dance of the angels," both visible and invisible worlds joining in the dance. This processional dance might be particularly suitable after reading Revelation 7:2-4, 9-14: "After this I looked, and behold, a great multitude which no man could number, from every nation, from all tribes and peoples and tongues, standing before the throne . . . "

"The Bread of Life," by Suzanne Toolan, sm, is a song that is sweeping in its affirmation of eternal life, and also lends itself well to simple congregational movement. People seem to naturally raise their arms on the chorus "And I will raise him up!" On the final chorus, which ends with " . . . on the last day," I have seen congregations spontaneously converge toward the center, arms still lifted. I would add one suggestion: on the final verse, ("Yes,

Lord, I believe that you are the Christ, the Son of God, who has
come into the world") ask everyone to kneel in place, holding
this position until the chorus begins. Then, when all rise and raise
their arms the contrast from low to high, or death to resurrection,
will be sensed vividly.

"God Is Love." Perhaps the occasion will call for the communion of saints of the living to be emphasized. A ritual sequence
might be organized to establish the universality of God's kingdom.
Begin with Gerard Manley Hopkins's beautiful lines from "As
Kingfishers Catch Fire":

> . . . For Christ plays in ten thousand places,
> Lovely in limbs, and lovely in eyes not his
> To the Father through the features of men's faces.

Ask all to bring in slides or photographs either of themselves
or of people from all around the world. The photographs could
be arranged at the entrance or around the church and the slides
shown to complement a reading such as 1 John 2:9-14 or 1 John
3:1-4.

At some point a circle dance would be done to encourage all
to look at one another in the present reality unselfconsciously
and with love. The following is a simple dance format based on
Father Clarence Rivers's "God is Love." Two concentric circles
are formed. The inside circle joins hands with their backs to the
center. On the chorus ("God is love, and he who abides in love,
abides in God, and God in him"), all move slowly around, the
inside circle moving in the opposite direction from the outside.
This will allow the people in each circle to slowly scan the faces
of those in the other circle as they pass by. On each verse the
circles stop and all join hands with one or two of the persons
they are facing in the other circle. Each of these little groupings
turns around in place in a warm, spontaneous manner, ending
back in the circle from which they began. This pattern is continued until the final chorus. On the final chorus all stand still and
sing, arms around each other's shoulders.

A Final Note

How does dance serve the church? Briefly: its mission is "explaining" mysteries, revealing new dimensions of scripture, witnessing to the *beauty* of God and creating faith-movement responses for community participation, enabling all to experience, with dancers, the power of body and spirit working harmoniously in praise of God.

Dance's gift in revelation is that by its unique, nonverbal interactions of spirit and body it can capture the nonverbal movements of the Holy Spirit in its interaction with people, as it groans within them, moves through scripture and manifests itself in the mysteries of the liturgy. Dance can externalize these movements. It makes them visible through the vehicle of the human body, drawing people into the mysteries through the use of basic, nonliteral materials. These include rhythms, dynamics, shapes, subtle and heightened creations of moods and feelings. I think of dance, and all the arts, as bridges between the visible and the invisible world of the spirit.

Dance serves to build a sense of community in congregations. Worshipers are elevated and drawn together through their common perception of the dance's portrayal. To reveal the inner and subtle movements of God's expressions, the dancer should attempt to attain a disciplined transparency, to be a clear vehicle, so as to minimize distractions from the spiritual purpose. The dancer also needs spiritual discipline to perceive with clarity the word of God. A dancer is aided by rapport with the congregation and should be dancing *with* and *for* them, not *to* them. Together they can then be lifted by the wings of the spirit to experience more clearly the kingdom. When subsequently the congregation is led in communal dances the experience is one of rejuvenation and delight in shared interplay of movement in relation to God. For example, rhythmic circle dances of all cultures are extremely powerful in drawing people together in celebration.

147

Sacred dance is a movement response from the heart to the living God. Dancers often create their initial sacred dances at a time of intensity which turns their hearts and souls to God. Overflowing from this inner experience, movements become ways of expressing what is occurring internally. Often this formative experience is the foundation for later dances. Each subsequent dance need not be drawn from such an experience of God's love, but a process has begun—a vocation has started which involves turning life's experiences into dances expressing the inner and outer dimensions of the soul's contacts with God.

It is a touch of grace if a dance comes easily. Usually, there is more hard work than is ever imagined. The work consists of refining and carefully integrating all the series of movements throughout the dance, and of polishing and practicing all the transitional steps so that the final dance is luminous, clear and retains a sense of spontaneity. But the joy of having a beautiful form for the spirit to play upon makes the effort all worthwhile.

The community's role

I am very grateful for the opportunities given to me to express my love of dance as a way of prayer in the evolving modes of worship in the church. I do what I do not to see far-reaching results, but because dance is close to a deep, free part of me that naturally seeks expression and finds it.

The need for dance is evident and the people are more and more ready for it. Since trained dance leaders interested in liturgy are few, dancers must be sought after and encouraged to direct their time and talents in this direction by a worshiping, loving and creative community.

My first dance at N.Y.U. in 1967 was preceded by a whole summer of experimentation dancing the gospels in the streets of New York City with a small band of friends. It was one of the most valuable and creative times of my life, and still indirectly affects what I do. We involved people in the gospel stories, often handing out bread and honey in conclusion as we ate together. This was inspired by a fearless Christian friend with a wild sense of adventure and fun and trust in God. It was his enthusiastic life of prayer that created the community and got me started— opening me to a new reality of communion with people other than dancers.

Other potential liturgical dancers need support and encouragement as they go through initiation into more whole, less compartmentalized ways of living their lives as they unite their dance and prayer.

The influence of dance on worship is only beginning to unfold.

THE LITURGICAL CONFERENCE

The Liturgical Conference is a voluntary nonprofit association of Christians, chiefly in the United States and Canada, who belong to different churches and confessional traditions but who have a common interest and concern: seeking to help all the churches celebrate public worship (liturgy) in ways that will express and nourish the faith community and that will speak to human needs.

Beginning in 1940 as an association of Roman Catholics, The Liturgical Conference has been since then and continues to be an educational, a motivating, and an advocacy force in Christian renewal, holding to the central and key role of liturgy in any faith community—but never in isolation from the general formation and education of that community, its mission, its witness to social justice and peace.

The Liturgical Conference endeavors to express needs that people feel and, with the help of its members, tries to share the resources and experience that correspond to those needs. Anyone who shares its concerns for liturgical authenticity and vitality is eligible for membership, at $25 per year, which includes a subscription to its bimonthly membership journal, *Liturgy*.

Members of The Liturgical Conference elect a board of directors (three year terms; one-third of the directors elected each year), which meets semiannually to set the policies of the association and to approve its projects. Its office and staff are located at the address below in Washington, D.C., implementing Conference projects and serving members' needs.

Further information as well as the resources listed below can be obtained from The Liturgical Conference, 1221 Massachusetts Ave., N.W., Washington, D.C. 20005 (prices subject to revision):

Periodicals
Liturgy, bimonthly journal for members of The Liturgical Conference (see above)
Homily Service—An Ecumenical Resource for Sharing the Word, monthly, $31/year
Living Worship, monthly, ten times a year, $6/year

Books (unless "kit," "packet," or cassette is indicated)
This Far by Faith—American Black Worship and Its African

Roots (proceedings of the Conference on Worship and Spirituality in the Black Perspective held in Washington, February 1977; a joint publication with the National Office for Black Catholics), $7.95

Strong, Loving and Wise—Presiding in Liturgy, by Robert W. Hovda, $8.25

Liturgy Committee Handbook, ed. by Virginia Sloyan, $5.25

The Lector's Guide, ed. by Gabe Huck and Virginia Sloyan, $4.75

The Ministry of Music, by William A. Bauman, $6.95. Combined book and companion cassette, $12.95

There Are Different Ministries—Guide for Acolytes, Ministers of Communion, Ushers and Occasional Ministers, by Robert W. Hovda, $4.95

From Ashes to Easter—Design for Parish Renewal (kit of materials for Lent as reinitiation for all), by Virginia Sloyan and Robert W. Hovda, $25

The Rite of Penance, Vol. I—Understanding the Document, by Ralph Keifer and Frederick R. McManus, $7.00

The Rite of Penance, Vol. II—Implementing the Rite, ed. by Elizabeth McMahon Jeep, $7.25

The Rite of Penance, Vol. III—Background and Directions, ed. by Nathan Mitchell, o.s.b., $8.95 (to be published November 1977)

The Rites of People—Exploring the Ritual Character of Human Experience, by Gerard A. Pottebaum, $5.50

Dry Bones—Living Worship Guides to Good Liturgy, by Robert W. Hovda, $5.70

Children's Liturgies, ed. by Virginia Sloyan and Gabe Huck, $10.25

Signs, Songs & Stories—Another Look at Children's Liturgies, ed. by Virginia Sloyan, $8.00

Celebrating Baptism, by Robert W. Hovda, 60¢

Meetings

North American Liturgical Week, annual three-day gathering of members and other interested persons: theme for 1977: "The Church as a Ministering Community"

Workshops (available to local sponsors: dioceses, churches, groups)

The Spirit Moves—A Workshop in Dance and Prayer—Ms. Carla De Sola

Presiding in Liturgy—Rev. Robert W. Hovda

Preaching from the New Lectionary—Rev. Hoyt L. Hickman

Proclaiming the Word: The Lector's Role—Rev. Gerard S. Sloyan

Sharing Sunday's Scriptures (Method for Group Process)—Ms. Mary C. Maher

Children's Liturgies—Ms. Elizabeth McMahon Jeep

Storytelling for Worship—Robert Bela Wilhelm, Th.D.

Celebrating the Major Feasts and Seasons of the Year—Mr. Gabe Huck

The Liturgy of the Hours in Parish and Religious Life—Rev. Andrew Ciferni, o.praem.

Planning Music as an Integral Dimension of Liturgy—Mr. Grayson W. Brown

Environment and the Visual Arts in Worship—Mr. Frank Kacmarcik, Mr. Robert Rambusch, or Rev. Mr. Willy Malarcher

Liturgy Committees: The Art of Planning Good Liturgical Worship—Mr. Gabe Huck or Rev. G. Thomas Ryan

From Ashes to Easter: Design for Parish Renewal—Rev. Robert W. Hovda or Rev. G. Thomas Ryan

Religious faith has always called forth in people the need to
find expression for feelings that words cannot contain. Carla
De Sola describes sacred dance as "an enfleshment of the
spirit in movement to God." In this volume are collected a
wide variety of carefully choreographed movement-
prayers for small groups and large, young and old, trained
dancers and those discovering the beauty of gesture in prayer
for the first time.

Carla De Sola is director of the Omega Liturgical Dance
Company, in residence at the Cathedral Church of St. John
the Divine in New York City, and regular dance columnist
for *Liturgy* magazine.

The Liturgical Conference
1221 Massachusetts Ave., N.W., Washington, D.C. 20005

ISBN 0-918208-04-1